HBR
DAILY
LEADER

HBR DAILY LEADER

Everyday Wisdom for

Exceptional Leadership

Harvard Business Review Press
Boston, Massachusetts

Printed and bound in India by Thomson Press India Ltd.

10 9 8 7 6 5 4 3 2

Library of Congress Cataloging-in-Publication Data

Names: Harvard Business Review Press, issuing body.
Title: HBR daily leader : everyday wisdom for exceptional leadership.
Other titles: Harvard business review daily leader | Harvard Business Review.
Description: Boston, Massachusetts : Harvard Business Review Press, [2024]
Identifiers: LCCN 2024017368 (print) | LCCN 2024017369 (ebook) |
    ISBN 9781647829797 (hardcover ; alk. paper) | ISBN 9781647829803 (epub)
Subjects: LCSH: Leadership.
Classification: LCC HD57.7 .H391385 2024 (print) | LCC HD57.7 (ebook) |
    DDC 658.4/092—dc23/eng/20240418
LC record available at https://lccn.loc.gov/2024017368
LC ebook record available at https://lccn.loc.gov/2024017369

ISBN: 978-1-64782-979-7
eISBN: 978-1-64782-980-3

The paper used in this publication meets the requirements of the American National Standard for Permanence of Paper for Publications and Documents in Libraries and Archives Z39.48-1992.

Make Your Leadership Growth an Everyday Habit

You have many identities in life, both professional and personal: Boss. Coach. Manager. Partner. Friend. Peer. Volunteer. Expert. Advocate. Educator. You may be in an early or a late phase of your career; your job title may indicate a senior or a junior position; you may manage people or not.

But you are a leader.

You get to define leadership for yourself: How will you show up? How will you present yourself? What values and purpose will guide you, and what will you model for the folks around you? You might find that you make major or minor changes to your definition, depending on which role you're in.

As a leader, you make decisions every day. You face tricky situations. You launch initiatives. You assess risk. You achieve great successes. You sometimes fail. Yet how often do you pause to consider what your day has taught you—how you can learn from the wins and the setbacks you've experienced? In a harried life with a packed schedule, it's hard to dedicate time for intentional learning. To make your own personal and professional growth a daily priority and practice. To set aside time to reflect, to find inspiration, to explore and be curious. The *HBR Daily Leader* helps you put your own development on your agenda in a consistent and purposeful way, every day. Carefully drawn from the best of the *Harvard Business Review* archives, this collection provides leadership wisdom to spark your thinking, quotations to inspire you, and questions to encourage deep reflection. Each day it addresses topics that challenge you with advice and expertise from authors you trust and from authors whose voices may be new to you.

HBR Daily Leader makes investing in your professional development easier. Whether you're still exploring who you are and where you want to go or you've landed the role of your dreams, this collection will provide 365 concise insights to help you ask—and answer—provocative questions, find your focus, and discover what leadership means to you.

How to Use This Book

Start anytime. Start on the first day of a new year. Start on your birthday. Start on the first day of your new job. Start as you prepare for your annual performance review. Start now. Commit to the first 30 days and then notice how quickly your habit forms. Look for improvements in your focus, productivity, self-awareness, and strategic thinking. We're sure you'll find them.

Whenever you choose to start, we recommend that you read just one insight each day. If the idea piques your interest, you can go deeper and read the full article at HBR.org. We've conducted surveys and combed research to identify the topics that matter most to leaders like you. We've distilled each day's wisdom on leadership and managing yourself topics in a way that is both succinct and satisfying.

These everyday wisdoms are not flash-in-the-pan trends. They're not hacks or stats. They're not an empty brain snack that will wear off within minutes, like the rush and crash of coffee or candy. The *HBR Daily Leader* offers research, insights, and practical advice to help you better manage your team, your business, and yourself.

Whether you've been gifted this book by someone who believes in your potential, or you've purchased it to help set and make progress on your goals, use it to elevate your performance. Every day has something to offer you. Draw inspiration from the quotations. Learn something new. Take a different perspective. Pause and use your favorite journaling tool to reflect more deeply on the questions posed.

Consciously devoting time to your own development is often difficult. Carving out a week or a month for a conference or a class can be challenging. But you can find time each day to consume one page that will propel your thinking and learning. Read the entry with your morning beverage before skimming headlines or scrolling social media. Make the most of your time while you wait for public transportation. Use it to set an intention for your day. Share the daily insight with your team to kick-start meetings. Create a new ritual by reading it as you review the progress you've made that day and think through your top to-dos for the following morning.

Return each day to discover, think, learn, imagine, and reflect. Not every insight will be new to you, but we hope that you'll find the right message at the right time. And, just as reading a favorite novel at different points in your life can imbue the same text with new meaning, returning to this collection year after year will spark fresh ideas according to your evolving context.

With the everyday wisdom of *HBR Daily Leader* as your touchstone, you can become an even more exceptional leader.

HBR
DAILY
LEADER

To Keep Learning, Stay Humble

When you're young, the people you learn from are smarter than you: parents, teachers, bosses. But by the time you reach a leadership role, there's a good chance that you're one of the smartest people in the room. Seeing yourself this way can feel good, but it will limit your growth if you think as you did earlier in your career that only people who are more intelligent than you have something to teach you. To continue developing, seek out and listen to ideas from others, especially people whose views and background differ from your own. A humble eagerness to learn from everybody means your learning opportunities will be unlimited.

Adapted from "How Will You Measure Your Life?," by Clayton M. Christensen

Improve Your Critical Thinking Skills

What helps you make good decisions? Critical thinking. What doesn't help? Accepting the first proposed solution or not taking the time to evaluate a topic from all sides. To guard against these blunders, question your assumptions—especially when the stakes are high. If you're coming up with a new business strategy, ask: Why is this the best way forward? What does the research say about our expectations for the future of the market? Also consider whether the logic and conclusions of an argument are supported by data. And seek out fresh perspectives, since it's tempting to rely on your inner circle. Get outside your bubble and ask different people to challenge your logic.

Adapted from "3 Simple Habits to Improve Your
Critical Thinking," by Helen Lee Bouygues

Leadership Means Interdependence, Not Independence

New managers often fail, at least initially, because they have misconceptions about what it means to be a boss. One of these myths is that your newfound status gives you the freedom to do what you want to for the company. Instead, you tend to find that your role is defined by interdependencies—by relationships with your employees, superiors, peers, and others inside and outside the company. All of them have their own goals, needs, and priorities, which may conflict with yours. To lead well, give up the idea of "freedom," and focus on building effective relationships. You'll ensure your team has the connections and support to succeed—which means you will, too.

Adapted from "Becoming the Boss,"
by Linda A. Hill

To Lead Better, Sleep More

When you don't get enough sleep, your judgment, self-control, and creativity suffer. You're more likely to be impatient, irritable, and antagonistic. But your fatigue hurts your relationships with employees too—and you're likely oblivious to these effects, according to researchers from Indiana University and the University of Washington. Employees of sleep-deprived leaders may be less engaged and behave less ethically. The takeaway? When you don't feel rested, your whole team pays the price. To get more sleep, consider how damaging your fatigue can be, not only to you but also to the people you lead.

How are your sleep habits affecting your team—in good ways or bad ones?

Adapted from "Sleep Well, Lead Better,"
by Christopher M. Barnes

How to Lose Well

Pivot

As a leader, you're focused on winning. But no one is successful all the time; you need to learn to lose with grace. One approach is to change your field of competition. If a project or initiative doesn't work out, step back and think about a new avenue for your efforts. What worked well in what you tried? How could you apply those skills, innovations, or ideas in a new way? Maybe there's another problem that needs solving that your work would be a perfect fit for. Don't let a failure be the end of your creative thinking.

———————

Adapted from "Good Leaders Lose with Grace,"
by Tim Leberecht

Leading in the Age of AI

"[Is] leadership . . . radically different in the AI age? No, but there are two key distinctions. First, leaders' hard skills will continue to be eclipsed by smart machines, while their soft skills will become ever more important. Second, while timeless leadership traits like integrity and emotional intelligence will no doubt remain important, leaders in the AI age need to be humble about others' contributions, adaptable to the challenges that get thrown into their paths, steadfast in their vision of the ultimate destination on this path, and constantly engaged with the changing world around them."

Adapted from "As AI Makes More Decisions, the Nature of Leadership Will Change," by Tomas Chamorro-Premuzic, Michael Wade, and Jennifer Jordan

Rethink Dedication

People no longer settle for jobs or companies that take over their lives, so adjust your view of dedication—or risk losing your top talent. Expand your idea of ambition and disconnect performance from time: If work is getting done well, it shouldn't matter how many hours people are at their desks. Don't hold employees to outdated standards, including ones from your early career. Let your people define passion for themselves and give them flexibility to work in ways that are best for them. Showing that you value what matters to your people will boost motivation—and retention.

Adapted from "How to Motivate Employees When Their
Priorities Have Changed," by Kristi Hedges

Three Principles of Work That People Love

"Creating a place where all people can find love in their work means incorporating three principles in everything your business does: *The people are the point*. Employees, rather than customers or shareholders, are the most important stakeholders in your organization. *One size fits one*. Each of those employees is a unique person with distinct loves, interests, and skills. *In trust we grow*. For employees to discover and contribute their loves at work, leaders must explicitly make trust the foundation of all practices and policies."

Adapted from "Designing Work That People Love,"
by Marcus Buckingham

What Derails Collaboration?

When you're planning collaborative, cross-functional projects, you may focus on logistics, processes, incentives, or outcomes. That makes perfect sense. But don't forget to consider how the groups you're asking to work together might experience the request—especially when you're telling them to break down walls, share information, sacrifice autonomy, split resources, or even cede responsibilities that define them. Those kinds of demands can make teams feel insecure and trigger defensive behaviors.

When you're leading cross-functional projects, how can you help teams feel less threatened?

Adapted from "The Collaboration Blind Spot,"
by Lisa B. Kwan

How to Make Your Employees Quit

Constrain Processes

Losing an employee hurts morale and productivity, and replacing people who leave is expensive. One mistake that can lead your people to quit is having too many process constraints. If employees have to wait for other people to provide the information or resources they need to do their own jobs, productivity suffers and frustration sets in. When you're discussing people's performance, have open conversations about what's getting in their way and how you can help. It may be that they need you to address a bottleneck with another department or leader. Using your influence to clear out roadblocks is good for morale—and work quality.

Adapted from "8 Things Leaders Do That Make
Employees Quit," by Jon Christiansen

Questions to Ask Often

How Can I Help?

When you ask great questions, you inspire curiosity, creativity, and deeper thinking in yourself and in your employees. One useful question is "How can I help?" Wanting to support others is admirable, but often we don't stop to think about the best way to do it; we just swoop in and try to save the day. So when your employee is complaining about an issue or expressing frustration, don't offer solutions—ask "How can I help?" This forces the person to think clearly about the problem and define it, which is the first step toward their owning and solving it.

Adapted from "5 Questions Leaders Should Be Asking
All the Time," by James E. Ryan

Develop a Strategy for Your Career

Calculate Your Timeline

To ensure a meaningful career, create a long-term strategy for it. One step is to figure out how long you'll be working. That may sound simple, but most people underestimate how long a career lasts. How many more years (and even months) do you expect to work? What's the average retirement age in your country? In your industry? What other factors, such as your health or family members', could affect your timeline? Will you have enough savings to live on, or will you need to (or want to) work part-time after retiring? Questions like these can help focus your long-term planning.

Adapted from "Developing a Strategy for a Life of Meaningful Labor," by Brian Fetherstonhaugh

Being the Boss ... of Your Friends

When you're promoted to a role above people you're friends with, things can get awkward. You want to maintain those relationships, but you also have to make decisions that favor the team's interests over any one employee's. To manage this awkwardness, speak candidly with your friends about how your role has changed and what expectations come with it. Acknowledge that things will get uncomfortable at times. Explain that you value their friendship, but you have to treat everyone equally and can't play favorites. Then follow through: If, for instance, you're going out to lunch, invite everyone, not just your friends. If employees suspect someone is getting preferential treatment, they may start to resent you or your friends.

Adapted from "What to Do When You Become Your Friend's Boss,"
by Benjamin Laker, Charmi Patel, Ashish Malik, and Pawan Budhwar

Reframe Tough Problems

"Research conducted by us and others shows that leaders and their teams devote too little effort to examining and defining problems before trying to solve them. . . . By jumping immediately into problem-solving, teams limit their ability to design innovative and durable solutions. When we work with organizations and teams, we encourage them to spend more time up front on *problem-framing*, a process for understanding and defining a problem. Exploring frames is like looking at a scene through various camera lenses while adjusting your angle, aperture, and focus."

What frames could you use to see problems in new ways?

———————

Adapted from "To Solve a Tough Problem, Reframe It,"
by Julia Binder and Michael D. Watkins

Don't Let Stress Stifle Your Creativity

When you're stressed out, producing new ideas can feel impossible. To get yourself unstuck, take a breath and relax; stop forcing yourself to be creative. Instead of thinking, "I must be creative right now," tell yourself, "I'm going to play around with some ideas." Then let your mind wander; taking a walk or napping naturally loosens up your brain. If you still feel stuck, give yourself more material to work with: Read about the topic you're tackling or talk to more-experienced colleagues. Above all else, give yourself time. You'll have a better chance of success when you let creative thoughts percolate.

Adapted from "How to Be Creative When You're Feeling Stressed," by Elizabeth Grace Saunders

Transition to Senior Leadership

Become an Agenda Setter

When you shift from leading a function to leading an enterprise, you must navigate a tricky set of changes in your leadership focus and skills. One change is becoming an agenda setter. You were promoted to the senior level because you could fix problems. Now, though, your task is to prioritize which problems the organization should tackle. You'll need to delegate well, rely on your team for guidance, and use your company's annual planning process to define key goals. But stay the course—learning to navigate uncertain, ambiguous environments can be overwhelming, and there's no better teacher than experience.

Adapted from "How Managers Become Leaders,"
by Michael D. Watkins

Your Team Needs the Right Mix of Personalities

Team composition is usually based on people's skills, but personality types are equally critical. For example, your employees may be:

- **Results-oriented:** people who organize work and take charge

- **Relationship-focused:** people who make real connections and are attuned to others' feelings

- **Process followers:** people who are reliable, detail-oriented, and conscientious

- **Innovative thinkers:** people who are curious, imaginative, and open to new ideas

- **Pragmatic:** people who are practical, prudent, and level-headed

If your team has only a few personality types, the group dynamic may be unbalanced and unproductive. When you're adding people to your team, consider their personality type and how it will add to, or detract from, a coherent mix.

Adapted from "Great Teams Are About Personalities, Not Just Skills,"
by Dave Winsborough and Tomas Chamorro-Premuzic

What Are You Working Toward?

As long as you're a leader, you must be able to answer this question: What are we here for? Responsibilities change, strategies evolve, and people are promoted and fired. Through it all, you need a consistent view of what you're working toward and why, especially in volatile times. Simply maintaining the status quo isn't enough. Being able to articulate a common purpose will help you both envision the future and chart a compelling path forward.

How do you build a strong, shared sense of meaning for everyone you work with?

Adapted from "How the Best Leaders Answer
'What Are We Here For?,'" by Margaret Heffernan

What Builds Trust?

To trust you, people need to see you demonstrate three things:

- **Empathy:** that you care about them

- **Logic:** that you're capable of meeting their needs

- **Authenticity:** that you can be expected to do what you say you'll do

When you wobble on one of these three dimensions, it's harder to build—or maintain—as much trust as you could.

How are you demonstrating your empathy, logic, and authenticity to your employees, peers, senior leaders, and customers?

Adapted from "10 Pitfalls That Destroy Organizational Trust," by Frances X. Frei and Anne Morriss

Don't Underestimate How Much Your Boss Wants to Know

"How much information a boss needs about what [you're] doing will vary significantly depending on the boss's style, the situation [they're] in, and the confidence the boss has in [you]. But it is not uncommon for a boss to need more information than [you] would naturally supply or for [you] to think the boss knows more than [they] really do. Effective managers recognize that they probably underestimate what their bosses need to know and make sure they find ways to keep them informed through processes that fit their styles."

Adapted from "Managing Your Boss,"
by John J. Gabarro and John P. Kotter

21

Leading as Your Team Grows

Context Switching

As your team grows, your processes and approach must evolve in several ways. One is by embracing context switching. Before, you could spend long, focused blocks of time on solving problems with your team. Now, your days are fragmented: lots of people, working on lots of projects, all of which require your attention and support. That means context switching—mentally shedding your last meeting's topic and preparing for the next—is one of your core tasks. It can feel overwhelming, so make good use of productivity tools to stay on top of things. And find pockets of time to step back and reflect to refresh your mind when you need it.

Adapted from "As Your Team Gets Bigger, Your Leadership Style Has to Adapt," by Julie Zhuo

What to Learn Next

How to Create Value

Great leaders never stop learning, but how do you know what skill you should work on next? One approach is to choose something that will help your team, unit, or company create more value. Think about what areas or processes could be improved, and what kinds of relevant knowledge you could gain about them. For example, if you're in operations, studying how to better manage large client projects could help reduce delivery times, or becoming more knowledgeable about sourcing materials could help reduce expenses. If you need ideas, talk to your team and colleagues about what they're struggling with; then look for training materials or courses to get started.

Adapted from "How to Decide What Skill to Work On Next,"
by Erika Andersen

Can You Think Like Your Competitors?

Your company's rivals are always trying to find and exploit your firm's vulnerabilities, so you should do the same. Try a simple strategic exercise with your employees. Create two teams. Team A lists your company's strengths, Team B its weaknesses. Then have the teams swap lists. Now, ask Team B to argue that the strengths are actually threats; Team A argues that the weaknesses are opportunities. Discuss the results and how everyone arrived at their conclusions. Next, repeat the exercise for your top competitors' strengths and weaknesses. The goal is to open your and your employees' eyes to new strategic possibilities.

Adapted from "Are Your Company's Strengths Really Weaknesses?," by Adam Brandenburger

Fight Your Perfectionism with Rules

Perfectionism can hold you back from the excellence you're striving for. For example, making decisions might paralyze you because the decisions all feel monumental. Mitigate your self-destructive tendencies by using rules to keep them in check. To stop ruminating over a decision, establish a rule that once you've thought about it three times, you'll make a call and move forward. To tone down your tendency to overdeliver, decide in advance that for certain types of work, "good enough" truly will be good enough. By becoming more aware of how perfectionism becomes a trap, you can create rules to help yourself escape it.

Adapted from "Don't Let Perfection Be the Enemy
of Productivity," by Alice Boyes

Don't Give Up on DEI

Sticking to DEI goals over the long term can be a considerable challenge, due to pressures from both inside your company (lack of budget or prioritization) and outside it (economic uncertainty, political conflict). To bring advocates and critics together, focus on the broader goal of creating conditions where all workers flourish. You'll need to cultivate four freedoms that allow everyone to bring their full humanity to work:

- The freedom for people to be their authentic selves

- The freedom to learn and grow and become their best selves

- The freedom to occasionally fade into the background

- The freedom to fail in ways that help them and their teams learn

What can you do to help these four freedoms take root on your team?

Adapted from "Where Does DEI Go from Here?,"
by Laura Morgan Roberts

Focusing as a Leader

On Others

One of your primary tasks as a leader is to direct attention. To do that, first learn to focus your own attention, in three broad ways: on yourself, on others, and on the wider world. Focusing on others means having—or building—the empathy to understand people's perspectives, feel what they feel, and sense what they need from you. It also means having the social sensitivity to build strong relationships—which gets harder as you rise through the ranks and gain power. Leaders who can do these tasks find common ground with others, offer opinions that carry great weight, and make others want to work with them.

Adapted from "The Focused Leader,"
by Daniel Goleman

Yes, You Can Manage Culture

"For better *and* worse, culture and leadership are inextricably linked. . . . Influential leaders often set new cultures in motion and imprint values and assumptions that persist for decades. . . . Unfortunately . . . it is far more common for leaders seeking to build high-performing organizations to be confounded by culture. Indeed, many either let it go unmanaged or relegate it to the HR function, where it becomes a secondary concern for the business. They may lay out detailed, thoughtful plans for strategy and execution, but because they don't understand culture's power and dynamics, their plans go off the rails. . . . It doesn't have to be that way. Our work suggests that culture can, in fact, be managed. The first and most important step leaders can take to maximize its value and minimize its risks is to become fully aware of how it works."

Adapted from "The Leader's Guide to Corporate Culture,"
by Boris Groysberg, Jeremiah Lee, Jesse Price,
and J. Yo-Jud Cheng

Write with Your Reader in Mind

To improve your writing, put yourself in your reader's shoes. Consider what information you'd want and what questions you'd have about the topic and let that guide you. Respect people's time by putting important information first and keeping your message as brief as possible. As for tone, picture your audience as intelligent novices: They're smart but they aren't experts, so avoid acronyms and jargon, and define technical terms. Focusing on what the reader needs will ensure people understand—and even look forward to—your writing.

Adapted from "4 Quick Tips to Improve Your Business Writing," by Lauren Brodsky

Two Misconceptions About Psychological Safety

Psychological safety is a core part of high-performing teams, so understanding what it is—and isn't—is essential. There are two common misconceptions. First, it's not about being "nice." There are many polite workplaces that don't have psychological safety because there's no candor, and people feel silenced by the enforced politeness. Second, psychological safety isn't about feeling comfortable all the time. In fact, learning, messing up, and pointing out mistakes is usually *uncomfortable*. But the ultimate goal is to help people take risks in a safe environment; doing so enables them to learn and grow and sets up your team for long-term success.

Have either of these misconceptions affected how you think about psychological safety?

Adapted from "What Is Psychological Safety?,"
by Amy Gallo

Questions to Ask Yourself

What's My Vision?

Through the ups and downs of your career, regularly asking yourself a few questions can help you stay on track with your goals and priorities. One of those questions is: How often and how well do you communicate a vision and priorities for your team? In the whirl of day-to-day activities, it can be hard to articulate the big picture and make sure your team understands it. But it's difficult to lead people if they don't know where to focus their efforts—or where they're going.

Do your employees know what you want them to do, and why, and how it will help build the company's future?

Adapted from "What to Ask the Person in the Mirror,"
by Robert Steven Kaplan

Being a Middle Manager Is Exhausting

Your position as a middle manager can be cognitively and emotionally draining because you play dual roles. You're more powerful than your employees, but less powerful than the senior executives you report to. That means you constantly vary your interaction styles (assertiveness versus deference) and are positioned between different stakeholder groups. This "vertical code-switching" takes a toll, from stress and anxiety to lower cognitive performance. You may not have the power to change these dynamics on your own, but becoming more aware of them can help you work with your boss to ease the burden.

Have you felt the pressures of vertical code-switching in your job?

Adapted from "Why Being a Middle Manager Is So Exhausting,"
by Eric M. Anicich and Jacob B. Hirsh

A Simple Way to Introduce Yourself

As a leader, you meet a lot of people. Introducing yourself quickly and effectively—without rambling on and on—is a challenge. An ideal introduction should be just a few sentences. Try the *present, past, future* framework to create yours.

- Start with a present-tense statement of your name and relevant details, such as your title or a project you're leading.

- Then use the past tense to establish your credibility. You could mention previous accomplishments or jobs, for example.

- Finally, show enthusiasm for what's in the future. You might say you're excited to partner with your audience or share your big goals for next quarter.

Present, past, future—it's that simple.

Adapted from "A Simple Way to Introduce Yourself,"
by Andrea Wojnicki

Why Do We Keep Promoting Incompetent Men?

"The problem . . . is not that we lack the means to spot incompetence, but that we more often choose to be seduced by it. . . . We have only ourselves to blame for our self-destructive leadership choices. Perhaps it is time to stop paying lip service to humility and integrity, until we practice what we preach and pick leaders on the basis of these traits. Instead of promoting people [based on] their charisma, overconfidence, and narcissism, we must put in charge people with actual competence, humility, and integrity. The issue is not that these traits are difficult to measure, but that we appear to not want them as much as we say."

Adapted from "How to Spot an Incompetent Leader,"
by Tomas Chamorro-Premuzic

Show Your Boss's Boss You Can Think Strategically

Your manager isn't the only executive who should know what you can do—show your boss's boss that you think strategically about the business. The next time you talk to them, ask questions that demonstrate your broad, long-term thinking. For example: "What milestones do you see the company hitting in five years? Ten years?" and "What industry trends should my team be responding to?" Or try: "How do you see my team's contributions evolving, given the company's strategic priorities?" Questions like these demonstrate to top decision-makers that you want to grow and add more value to the company.

Adapted from "How to Have a Successful Meeting
with Your Boss's Boss," by Melody Wilding

Present Your Data Clearly

Having a lot of data doesn't guarantee your presentation will be effective; you need to explain what the data means. Consider the main takeaway you want your audience to have and convey it in your talk ("This table shows . . ."). Don't make listeners decode the numbers themselves. You should also ensure your charts are readable both in person and in a virtual setting. The simpler your slides are, the better. And only present the data that truly supports your point. If you're illustrating a sales trend for the last two years, what happened three years ago may be irrelevant. Don't give your audience more numbers than they need.

Adapted from "Present Your Data Like a Pro,"
by Joel Schwartzberg

Yes, You Can Get Work Done Between Meetings

Too many meetings to tackle your to-do list? Rethink your approach. Break down big assignments into bite-size tasks you can complete when you have a few minutes. Keep a list of these small tasks and use it to make incremental progress. Ticking off even one or two items will move you toward the finish line. If you're still struggling to get things done, add "project time" to your calendar as a recurring event. For example, reserve an hour each morning for focused work. Protect these blocks of time and use them for important tasks you can't get done otherwise.

Adapted from "How to Get Your To-Do List Done When You're Always in Meetings," by Elizabeth Grace Saunders

Enjoy the Silence

"Taking time for silence restores the nervous system, helps sustain energy, and conditions our minds to be more adaptive and responsive to the complex environments in which so many of us now live, work, and lead. . . . But cultivating silence isn't just about getting respite from the distractions of office chatter or [notifications]. Real sustained silence, the kind that facilitates clear and creative thinking, quiets inner chatter as well as outer. This kind of silence is about resting the mental reflexes that habitually protect a reputation or promote a point of view."

Adapted from "The Busier You Are, the More You Need
Quiet Time," by Justin Zorn and Leigh Marz

Make It Safer to Talk About Mental Health

Employees struggling with mental health challenges should be able to ask for help without worrying that you'll look at them differently. Think about how to create a work environment that makes them feel safe enough to do so. For example, pay attention to the language your team uses. Comments like "Don't get all OCD on my spreadsheet" stigmatize issues that employees could be struggling with. Discourage that kind of language when you hear it, and if necessary, explain why it's hurtful. Familiarize yourself with your company's mental health resources and be ready to point team members to them.

Adapted from "5 Ways Bosses Can Reduce the Stigma of Mental Health at Work," by Diana O'Brien and Jen Fisher

Don't Be a Victim of Your Success

Curb Your Impatience

To keep performing at your best, you must overcome the barriers that accompany your success. One barrier is being impatient for results. Accomplished people can get used to solving problems and quickly moving on to the next one, but that approach doesn't work for big, intractable issues. When you test out new methods, gather feedback from others and iterate, or build consensus around the best way forward, impatience can be a trap—one that stands in the way of innovation, novel ideas, and communication.

How can you slow down when solving big problems to give great ideas time to grow?

Adapted from "Want to Change the World? Don't Let Your Own Success Get in the Way," by Rosabeth Moss Kanter

During Change, Ask Employees What They're Worried About

To lead a successful organizational change, you must communicate empathetically. That means finding out how your team feels about the change and tailoring your emails and meetings to their concerns. So talk to your team members about what's happening and why. Ask what they're worried about and what kind of improvements they'd like to see. Listen closely, and then address what you hear, being as transparent as you can. Repeat these steps during each phase of the change, so you can gauge how people's feelings are shifting over time. Your goal is to make sure everyone feels included and heard.

Adapted from "The Secret to Leading Organizational Change Is Empathy," by Patti Sanchez

Overcome Executive Isolation

Recognize the Signs

The loneliness you might feel as a senior leader may seem like a small price to pay for the rewards, recognition, and power. But being isolated can compromise your decision-making and effectiveness. One way to overcome this condition is to recognize its existence. So regularly reflect on whether you're starting to feel detached from others. Ask yourself: Are employees challenging your thinking, or just agreeing with you? Are you getting the full picture of situations, or just a filtered version? Are you seeking out the advice of trusted colleagues, or relying only on your own instincts?

Adapted from "How to Overcome Executive Isolation,"
by Ron Ashkenas

Your Employees Need Both Recognition and Appreciation

You may use the terms "recognition" and "appreciation" interchangeably, but employees need both, so it's helpful to understand the difference. Recognition is about giving positive feedback based on results or performance. That can happen formally (awards, promotions) or informally (verbal thank-yous, handwritten notes). Appreciation is about acknowledging a person's inherent value. The point isn't their accomplishments; it's their worth as a colleague and a human being. This distinction matters because if you focus solely on praising positive outcomes, on *recognition*, you miss out on opportunities to connect with and support your team members—to *appreciate* them. Recognition is important when someone has earned it. Appreciation is important all the time.

Adapted from "Why Employees Need Both Recognition and Appreciation," by Mike Robbins

Develop Your Learning Agility

Get Better at Receiving Feedback

If you rely on the same assumptions and behavioral repertoires you've used for years as a leader, you are prone to stagnate, underperform, or derail, according to research from Korn Ferry. The solution is to develop learning agility, the capacity for rapid, continuous learning. One method is to be less defensive when receiving feedback. When you have a track record of success, it's easy to downplay criticism or view issues as one-offs. Instead, stay open to what the feedback giver tells you. Don't argue with them—just listen. Embrace the view that you always have something new to learn, and that new perspectives are essential to your growth.

Adapted from "4 Ways to Become a Better Learner,"
by Monique Valcour

Your Elevator Pitch Should Grow with You

"Early in your career you may have been taught to hone an elevator pitch so that you could make the most of chance encounters with superiors or prospective employers. You were probably advised to have tightly scripted answers to questions such as 'What are you working on?' and 'What do you want to do?' As you move into a top position, you'll need a pitch that tackles the questions 'Who are you as a leader?' and 'What do you care most about?' You want to be predictable in the best sense of the word: someone whose values are unwavering and clear."

Adapted from "The Leap to Leader,"
by Adam Bryant

How Much Influence Do You Have at Work?

The amount of influence you have isn't always determined by your job title. Gauge your informal power by listing the top 10 people who help you get things done, and consider how much you depend on each of them (say, for career advice, emotional support, or access to stakeholders). Next, think about yourself from their perspectives. What do you uniquely offer them? Finally, look for red flags: Do your contacts help you more than you help them? Are they mostly in one business unit? If you're not satisfied with your audit's results, plan how you'll improve them, such as by contributing more across the company or spending more time with stakeholders.

Adapted from "How to Figure Out How Much Influence
You Have at Work," by Maxim Sytch

Better Succession Planning

Start Now

Succession planning is complex and important to the ongoing success of your company. Is your board proactive about succession planning? Maybe they've picked a replacement for the CEO but haven't fully developed them for the role; maybe succession is delegated to the current CEO. Neither approach is good enough. Succession planning should start the moment a new CEO is appointed. Directors should constantly monitor the leadership pipeline and adjust as needed. If there's no potential successor among the CEO's direct reports, look to the next level and consider development opportunities to help those executives progress. Preparing for your next leader now is the best way to support and secure the company's future when the time comes.

Adapted from "The High Cost of Poor Succession Planning," by Claudio Fernández-Aráoz, Gregory Nagel, and Carrie Green

Still Stewing About That Mistake You Made?

When you mess up, do you replay it in your head for days or even weeks? Ruminating this way can lead to serious anxiety. To break the cycle:

- **Identify your rumination triggers.** Do certain people, projects, or decisions make you second-guess yourself? Notice when (and why) a situation gets you overthinking.

- **Label negative thoughts and feelings as "thoughts" and "feelings."** Instead of saying "I'm inadequate," saying "I *feel* inadequate" puts distance between you and your reactions.

- **Distract yourself.** If nothing else works, take a walk, meditate, or fill out an expense report—any simple activity you can focus on for a few minutes.

Adapted from "How to Stop Obsessing Over Your Mistakes,"
by Alice Boyes

To Help Women Get Ahead

Give Them Development Opportunities

As a leader, you know that women are still dramatically under-represented in positions of power: Few *Fortune* 500 companies are led by women, and even fewer by women of color. One way to reduce the barriers holding women back is to give them chances to grow and develop. Make sure both men and women have access to stretch assignments and challenging projects, and that women aren't stuck with lower-status roles. Mentor and sponsor women to support their careers; even women seen as high potentials are less likely than men to be sponsored. Giving women and men equal opportunity to shine and grow and narrowing the gender gap should be a deliberate, ongoing process.

Adapted from "How to Close the Gender Gap,"
by Colleen Ammerman and Boris Groysberg

What Successful People Do

Get Specific and Seize Opportunities to Pursue Goals

Why have you been so successful in reaching some of your goals, but not others? Even brilliant, highly accomplished people aren't great at understanding why they succeed or fail. But successful people do a few things differently, according to decades of research on achievement. One is getting specific about goals. "Eat less" or "sleep more" don't really define success; "lose five pounds" or "be in bed by 10 p.m." are clear and precise. Relatedly, successful people notice and seize opportunities to pursue their goals. Decide when you will take specific actions: "On Mondays, I'll exercise for 30 minutes before work." This kind of planning will increase your chances of following through.

Adapted from "Nine Things Successful People
Do Differently," by Heidi Grant

Set Healthy Standards of Work for Your Team

When your employees feel too busy all the time, their creativity, drive, and job satisfaction are diminished. So create healthy standards of work for your team. Start by setting an example: Take lunch breaks, stop working at a reasonable hour, and don't send email late at night. You can also help people be smart with their time. Encourage them to block out time to finish up lingering projects, freeing up space on their to-do lists (and in their brains). And increase workload transparency by staying current on what everyone is working on. Then consider whether the team needs more resources or could stop doing certain kinds of work.

Adapted from "Preventing Busyness from Becoming Burnout," by Brigid Schulte

Storytelling to Drive Change

Understand Deeply, Describe Simply

When your organization needs to make a big change, stories can help you convey not only why it needs to transform but also what the future will look like in specific, vivid terms. Good storytelling does four things. One of them is understanding deeply while describing simply. No matter your professional background, if you can only describe something in complex or jargony language, you'll only reach other experts. Think about the change you want to lead, and ask yourself: Can you capture your vision in a page? A paragraph? A word? The simpler you can say it, the better.

Adapted from "Storytelling That Drives Bold Change,"
by Frances X. Frei and Anne Morriss

True Leaders Invite Dissent

"The best leaders I've studied—executives and entrepreneurs who have created enduring economic value based on sound human values—recognize and embrace the 'obligation to dissent.' . . . You can't be an effective leader in business, politics, or society unless you encourage those around you to speak their minds, to bring attention to hypocrisy and misbehavior, and to be as direct and strong-willed in their evaluations of you as you are in your strategies and plans for them."

Adapted from "True Leaders Believe Dissent Is an Obligation," by Bill Taylor

Why You Should Read More Fiction

Lots of leaders read, but many default to nonfiction. And while reading for knowledge is great, what fiction offers you is just as useful. Classic and contemporary works of fiction offer low-cost lessons in how to manage moral complexity—everything from voicing a nuanced position on a thorny topic to dealing with quandaries related to greed, self-deceit, or likability. Fictional characters routinely grapple with these and other issues, and struggle to make choices that are congruent with their values. That's why, especially when you're facing situations with no obvious right answer, their stories convey important lessons for your life and work.

Adapted from "Want to Be a Leader? Read
More Fiction," by Brooke Vuckovic

Break Your Career-Limiting Habit

Rethink Distance

We all have a career-limiting habit, such as procrastinating or using our phones when we should be connecting with others. But people who overcome bad habits take control of the circumstances that feed them, according to research from Crucial Learning. One way to do this is to be strategic about "distance." For example, if you need to overcome procrastination, do your focused work in a huddle room instead of an open office. If you want to read more industry news sites, put them on your homepage instead of in distracting social media feeds. Physically separate yourself from temptations, bring helpful things closer, and change your surroundings to support the behavior you want.

Adapted from "Trick Yourself into Breaking a
Bad Habit," by Joseph Grenny

What Great Questions Do

Show That You're Prepared

A great question can help you learn more about a task, unlock hidden opportunities, deliver better results, and mitigate unforeseen risks. One mark of a great question is it shows that you prepared for the conversation. Whatever the topic, demonstrate that you did your homework and know the topic's broader context. Context-specific questions invite others to share their expertise and propel the conversation forward. For example, don't ask, "What's our South America strategy?" Instead, ask, "I read that our top competitor is expanding in Brazil this year. How should that affect our South America strategy?"

Adapted from "The Art of Asking Great Questions,"
by Tijs Besieux

Great Mentors Choose Mentees Carefully

Sharing your knowledge and experience with someone is an investment you should make carefully. A good mentee is curious, organized, efficient, responsible, and engaged. If, on the other hand, a mentee expects you to do the work of keeping the mentoring relationship going, or insists on doing things their own way, that behavior may not bode well. Try testing their resolve with a simple task, like reading a book and returning to discuss it within a month, or joining you at a strategy session and writing up their observations. You'll get a sense of their thinking process, communication skills, and level of interest.

Adapted from "6 Things Every Mentor Should Do,"
by Vineet Chopra and Sanjay Saint

The Persuasive Power of Similarities and Compliments

People like people who like them. That's why, when you need to be persuasive, an effective approach is to find common ground or praise something you admire about the person. The similarities you share could be anything—a hobby, a sports team, parenthood. The important thing is to identify and establish that bond early, to help create goodwill and trustworthiness in your later encounters. When it comes to offering praise, tell the person what you value, such as their work ethic or how well they support their employees. A sincere, well-placed compliment, or a shared interest, can help win someone over and convince them of your good intentions.

Adapted from "Harnessing the Science of Persuasion,"
by Robert B. Cialdini

What's Your Leadership Style?

Authoritative

Your personal leadership style has a powerful impact on your organization. One type of leadership that has positive effects on an organization's working environment and results is the authoritative style. Authoritative leaders are visionaries who free their team to experiment and take risks. They motivate people by making clear how their work supports the larger strategy and giving feedback about how their performance furthers the vision. While the authoritative style is often effective, it can fail when a leader works with a team of experts or more experienced peers, or if their style becomes overbearing. As you lead, think about what style a situation calls for and whether your current approach is working well or may need an adjustment.

Adapted from "Leadership That Gets Results,"
by Daniel Goleman

59

Comparing Women with Men Holds Women Back

"Integrating leadership into one's core identity is particularly challenging for women, who must establish credibility in a culture that is deeply conflicted about whether, when, and how they should exercise authority. Practices that equate leadership with behaviors considered more common in men suggest that women are simply not cut out to be leaders. . . . Despite a lack of discriminatory intent, subtle, 'second-generation' forms of workplace gender bias can obstruct the leadership identity development of a company's entire population of women. . . . The resulting underrepresentation of women in top positions reinforces entrenched beliefs, prompts and supports men's bids for leadership, and thus maintains the status quo."

Adapted from "Women Rising: The Unseen Barriers,"
by Herminia Ibarra, Robin J. Ely, and Deborah M. Kolb

To Move On from Change

Think "Before" and "After"

Sometimes a big change—personal or professional—upends your identity. Making a distinct break with the past can help you move forward. Choose an event to serve as the separator of "before" and "after." It could be something big, like a health scare or the birth of a child; you may also just decide that when you wake up tomorrow, you'll embrace your new reality. Whatever you pick, mentally imbue it with significance, and consider telling a friend or colleague to give it more weight. Consciously deciding to move on can help you leave behind an identity that's no longer part of your life.

Adapted from "When a Major Life Change Upends Your Sense of Self," by Madeline Toubiana, Trish Ruebottom, and Luciana Turchick Hakak

Share Your Mistakes— and Your Lessons

To perform at their best, people need to know they won't be punished for errors. To build psychological safety on your team, show employees that making mistakes is allowed—and learning from them is encouraged. When your team members are struggling with setbacks, tell them about a time you fell short at work. Explain how the experience helped you develop as a leader, and what you did differently as a result. Also, talk about the fear, doubt, or embarrassment you felt after messing up, to help normalize those kinds of tough emotions. Emphasizing that failure often leads to growth will show employees they aren't expected to be perfect.

———————

Adapted from "What Is Psychological Safety?,"
by Amy Gallo

Trust, Not Your Title, Gives You Authority

New managers often fail, at least initially, because they have misconceptions about what it means to be a boss. One of these myths is that people listen to you because of the formal authority of your title. In fact, people will follow you because of three informal traits:

- **Character:** whether you do the right thing

- **Competence:** how well you support your team's success

- **Influence:** how you use resources and cross-functional relationships to get things done

Don't rely on your title alone to drive results; great employees are unlikely to simply follow orders. Instead, focus on building trust and credibility with peers and team members.

Adapted from "Becoming the Boss,"
by Linda A. Hill

How to Make Your Employees Quit

Set Inconsistent Goals

Losing an employee hurts morale and productivity, and replacing people who leave is expensive. One mistake that can lead your people to quit is setting inconsistent goals. When your employees are forced to choose between tasks to meet competing expectations—such as faster customer service versus logging customer information accurately—the result is a team of stressed-out people without clear priorities. Write down your team's goals and expectations and consider whether any contradictions or overlaps exist. Next, make necessary changes and share them with the team. This exercise will give your team more stability and more control over their tasks.

Adapted from "8 Things Leaders Do That Make
Employees Quit," by Jon Christiansen

Disentangle Competition from Strategy

One paradox of strategy? Companies tend to favor incrementally improving their current products over creating new markets or industries. Yet the latter strategy usually provides more return on investment. Part of the problem is that we think *competition* is inherently tied to *strategy*—that outperforming rivals should be our main goal. Competition *is* important, but so is looking for entirely new ideas and market spaces. When you're leading brainstorming or innovation sessions, don't just focus on improving what you're already doing. Push your team to find opportunities that no one has thought of yet. The best kind of competition happens in spaces where no one else is competing.

Adapted from "Blue Ocean Strategy,"
by W. Chan Kim and Renée Mauborgne

The Link Between Progress and Motivation

"Of all the things that can boost emotions, motivation, and perceptions during a workday, the single most important is making progress in meaningful work. . . . The more frequently people experience that sense of progress, the more likely they are to be creatively productive in the long run. Whether they are trying to solve a major scientific mystery or simply produce a high-quality product or service, everyday progress—even a small win—can make all the difference in how they feel and perform."

Take five minutes at the end of your day to write down three things you did that you're proud of, to track incremental progress toward your goals.

Adapted from "The Power of Small Wins,"
by Teresa M. Amabile and Steven J. Kramer

Help Your Leadership Team Fight Well

Having a good fight on your leadership team is a challenge. Personalities can become entwined with issues, and executives may struggle to balance rational decision-making and their emotions. Help your team argue as a team by focusing on the facts and data about an issue, not gut feelings. Consider multiple options and alternatives, widening the discussion and preventing narrow, either-or mindsets. Framing strategic choices as collaborative, rather than competitive, exercises is another way to prevent conflicts from turning personal. And don't overlook the power of simple jokes to lighten the mood—even forced humor can release tension and promote collaboration.

Adapted from "How Management Teams Can Have a Good Fight," by Kathleen M. Eisenhardt, Jean L. Kahwajy, and L. J. Bourgeois III

What Will You Regret Not Having Done?

Careers are rarely a straight line. It's likely that yours will move in a number of directions—some less obvious than others. To take stock of where you are and where you want to go, ask: Ten years from now, what will you miss not having done or learned? Think about subjects you'd like to study, interests you'd like to pursue, and places you'd like to go—both personally and professionally. Then consider your career progression and how you might incorporate these goals. Regularly reflecting this way, and aligning your priorities with current and future jobs whenever possible, will help ensure your career journey is a fulfilling one.

Adapted from "6 Questions to Ask at the Midpoint of Your Career," by Rebecca Knight

Transition to Senior Leadership

Shift from Specialist to Generalist

When you shift from leading a function to leading an enterprise, you must navigate a tricky set of changes in your leadership focus and skills. One change is becoming a generalist. No one is an expert in every function; it's tempting to overmanage the areas you know and undermanage others. But functions are distinct subcultures with their own mental models, languages, and tools. You need to know all of them—and be able to evaluate and recruit people to be experts when you aren't. Start by building relationships with colleagues in other functions so that you can support and learn from each other, and understand what excellence looks like in their area.

Adapted from "How Managers Become Leaders,"
by Michael D. Watkins

Make Time for Your Hobbies

Top leaders say that their leisure interests help them cope with the ever-increasing demands of their jobs, according to research from Vrije Universiteit Amsterdam. By investing considerable time in hobbies, personal interests, and volunteer gigs, and even blocking off time for them far in advance, the leaders in the study prevented work from becoming all-consuming. The benefits their hobbies bring are manifold, from providing lessons in humility, to strengthening their authentic identities, to helping them detach from work.

What leadership benefits do your hobbies offer you? How can you make more time for them?

Adapted from "Why CEOs Devote So Much Time to Their Hobbies," by Emilia Bunea, Svetlana N. Khapova, and Evgenia I. Lysova

When Work Is Overwhelming

Practice Acceptance

When you have too much to do, you may feel anxious any time you're not working. But a huge to-do list doesn't have to overwhelm you. One strategy for managing stress is to practice acceptance. The best self-talk is compassionate and helps you feel calmer and more in control. Try:

- "I can only focus on the thing I'm doing right now."

- "I would prefer to do more in a day, but I'll accept my realistic limits."

- "I enjoy my work, so I like to be busy. It's natural that I'll feel overwhelmed sometimes. I can handle those emotions and make adjustments as needed."

Adapted from "5 Things to Do When You Feel Overwhelmed by Your Workload," by Alice Boyes

Know Your Strengths, Know Your Weaknesses

"Taking responsibility for your career starts with an accurate assessment of your current skills and performance. Can you write down your two or three greatest strengths and your two or three most significant weaknesses? . . . This exercise involves meaningful reflection and, almost always, requires soliciting the views of people who will tell you the brutal truth. . . . Take control of this process by seeking coaching, asking for very specific feedback, and being receptive to input from a wide variety of people at various levels within your organization. This gathering of feedback needs to be an ongoing process because, as your career progresses, you will face new challenges and demands."

How can you make this process of gathering feedback a regular, sustainable practice?

Adapted from "Reaching Your Potential,"
by Robert Steven Kaplan

Learning to Learn

Go for More

Acquiring new knowledge quickly and continually is a skill that will never be obsolete. One way to do it is to increase your aspiration. When we're confronted with a learning opportunity, we often focus on the negative—*This will take too long* or *My current method works fine*—which decreases our motivation. Instead, make yourself more eager to learn by focusing on what you'll gain. Picture the tangible benefits of the skill, such as understanding customer behavior more clearly or being able to solve problems in a new way. By orienting your mindset around how you'll put the knowledge into practice, you can motivate yourself to learn almost anything.

Adapted from "Learning to Learn,"
by Erika Andersen

Your Leadership Voice

Built on Character

Cultivating your leadership voice requires building the capacity to respond authentically, constructively, and effectively, no matter the situation or audience. One aspect of your voice is character. It's rooted in the fundamental concepts that guide and motivate your actions. Principles such as "Give the benefit of the doubt" or "Be direct with respect" can serve as anchors, helping you avoid becoming a chameleon, giving into a fight-or-flight response, or treating people better when you have something to gain. Ultimately, a voice of character is about who you are, and who you choose to be.

How do you demonstrate your character with what you say and do?

Adapted from "You Don't Just Need One Leadership
Voice—You Need Many," by Amy Jen Su

Build Skills That AI Can't Copy

Develop Your Interpersonal Strengths

AI tools may compete with the lower and middle ends of many professions, such as copywriting and design. So it's critical to develop yourself in ways that AI can't copy. One way is to hone the soft skills that are so crucial to leadership. While machines try to show empathy or self-awareness ("I am sorry my answer upset you"), those responses are based on text prediction, not real feelings. As a human, you're wired to respond to emotion. Understanding what others think and feel, and being able to show it, will remain essential to thriving amid ever-greater technological advances.

Adapted from "5 Ways to Future-Proof Your Career in the Age of AI,"
by Dorie Clark and Tomas Chamorro-Premuzic

Help Your Employees Feel the Purpose in Their Work

Instilling purpose in your employees takes more than lofty speeches or mission statements. When done badly, those methods can trigger cynicism rather than commitment. To inspire and engage people, remember two things. First, purpose is a feeling. You could *tell* your team their work is important, but can you help them *feel* it? Find ways to show people the impact of their jobs, such as through customer testimonials. Second, authenticity matters. If your attempts at creating purpose don't align with your past behavior, your message will backfire. Suddenly caring about the impact of a product on a customer's quality of life after years of emphasizing quarterly profits, for example, could seem manipulative.

Adapted from "Helping Your Team Feel the Purpose
in Their Work," by Dan Cable

Just Because You're Bright Doesn't Mean You're Smart

"Far too many people—especially people with great expertise in one area—are contemptuous of knowledge in other areas or believe that being bright is a substitute for knowledge. First-rate engineers, for instance, tend to take pride in not knowing anything about people. Human beings, they believe, are much too disorderly for the good engineering mind. Human resources professionals, by contrast, often pride themselves on their ignorance of elementary accounting or of quantitative methods altogether. But taking pride in such ignorance is self-defeating. Go to work on acquiring the skills and knowledge you need to fully realize your strengths."

Adapted from "Managing Oneself,"
by Peter F. Drucker

Build Your Collaboration Skills

Internal Self-Awareness

Teams are interconnected systems of preferences, skills, experiences, and perspectives. To lead such a complex entity well, you must develop your *internal* self-awareness. Doing so involves reflecting on your feelings, beliefs, and values. Without that foundational understanding, you're more likely to see your beliefs as "the truth," and fail to see others' perspectives as equally valid. To build your internal self-awareness, ask a few questions in challenging situations:

- What emotions am I experiencing?

- What am I assuming about another person or the situation?

- What are the facts versus my interpretations?

- What are my core values, and how might they be impacting my reactions?

Pausing to reflect and consider possible responses can help you engage thoughtfully and productively.

Adapted from "To Improve Your Team, First Work on Yourself," by Jennifer Porter

Value Productivity, Not Busyness

Is it important to you that your employees seem busy all the time? If so, you may be creating a culture of overwork, where increased work doesn't necessarily lead to increased productivity. But you can reverse the destructive trend. Reward output rather than hours worked. Promote employees based on who produces the best results, regardless of how long they're at their desks. Next, foster deep work. Free up employees' time for high-value projects by delegating or eliminating their low-value tasks. Finally, model the right behavior. The best leaders aren't those who never leave the office. They're the ones who know which work matters most—and let themselves sign off when it's done.

Adapted from "Beware a Culture of Busyness,"
by Adam Waytz

When Growth Plateaus

Examine Your Environment

When you become a leader, it's easy for your growth to plateau. Your goals are more nebulous (manage a team, run a function), and endless requests for your time can steal attention from your top priorities. To continue growing, try optimizing your environment. Think about common physical distractions (such as checking your phone) and how to minimize them (say, leaving your phone behind and working elsewhere). Or improve your psychological environment by setting specific deadlines for yourself, even for projects without firm due dates. People with high self-control don't resist temptations with willpower alone, according to a Florida State University study: They change their environments to support their productivity.

Adapted from "3 Strategies for Holding Yourself Accountable,"
by Diana Kander

Demonstrate Your Strategic Thinking in Meetings

Being able to think strategically isn't enough—senior executives need to witness your thinking. Showcase your skills and ambition by bringing your point of view to meetings. Before a strategy meeting, for example, block out time to think through the agenda and prepare. Then find a moment in the meeting to share your perspective. Demonstrate that you've considered how other departments or the world will be affected by the issues at hand, so higher-ups see you aren't thinking in a vacuum. Leaders will know you're ready to be promoted when they know you can position the company for the future.

Adapted from "How to Demonstrate Your Strategic Thinking Skills," by Nina A. Bowman

Addressing Racism at Work

As intractable as it seems, racism in the workplace can be more effectively addressed with the right information, incentives, and investment. One important step you can take is to increase employees' empathy through education about racism's effects. Raise awareness and understanding through psychologically safe listening sessions; invite employees to share their own experiences if they feel comfortable doing so. Offer learning sessions that provide historical and scientific evidence of the persistence of racism, since employees might not think their company has a problem. Empathy is critical for making progress toward racial equity because, once people are aware of the problem, the next question is whether they care enough to do something about it.

Adapted from "How to Promote Racial Equity in the Workplace," by Robert Livingston

Power Corrupts. Humility Prevents That

The more powerful you are, the more you need humility, since it can stave off power's corrupting effects. To build humility, you can do a few things. First, make it acceptable, even desirable, to say "I don't know." Admitting you don't have all the answers builds trust and credibility and opens the door for employees to offer their expertise. Second, establish ways to get honest input from your people. Whether through team meetings, "ask me anything" forums, or frank one-on-one conversations, you need robust ways to get employees' unvarnished views. Power can insulate you from those you lead—don't let it.

Adapted from "Don't Let Power Corrupt You,"
by Julie Battilana and Tiziana Casciaro

What Building Competitive Advantage Means

"Keeping score of existing advantages is not the same as building new advantages. The essence of strategy lies in creating tomorrow's competitive advantages faster than competitors mimic the ones you possess today. . . . An organization's capacity to improve existing skills and learn new ones is the most defensible competitive advantage of all. . . . They must fundamentally change the game in ways that disadvantage incumbents: devising novel approaches to market entry, advantage building, and competitive warfare. For smart competitors, the goal is not competitive imitation but competitive innovation, the art of containing competitive risks within manageable proportions."

Adapted from "Strategic Intent,"
by Gary Hamel and C.K. Prahalad

To Help Women Get Ahead

Rethink Your Applicant Pools

As a leader, you know that women are still dramatically under-represented in positions of power: Few *Fortune* 500 companies are led by women, and even fewer by women of color. One way to reduce the barriers holding women back is to rethink your applicant pools. For starters, don't just rely on executives' networks or ask, "Who do we know who's good?"—that approach likely favors men. Go beyond your usual recruiting practices to identify overlooked applicants. And when writing job descriptions, avoid typically masculine terms, such as *competitive* and *forceful*; also avoid superlatives, such as *excellent coding skills* rather than simply *coding skills*. Using either may discourage women from applying.

Adapted from "How to Close the Gender Gap,"
by Colleen Ammerman and Boris Groysberg

Questions to Ask Yourself

How Am I Spending My Time?

Through the ups and downs of your career, regularly asking yourself a few questions can help you stay on track with your goals and priorities. One of those questions is: How are you spending your time? If what you're doing every day doesn't align with your major priorities, that's a problem. It's also a problem for your team, since employees take their time-management cues from you.

Which of the activities you're doing truly need your time? Which could be delegated to free you up for higher-value work?

Adapted from "What to Ask the Person in the Mirror,"
by Robert Steven Kaplan

Focus on What's Important, Not on What's Urgent

Scheduling

Your to-do list has both important and urgent tasks. It's easy to work on what's due soonest, but sometimes the important projects need your attention more. To prioritize what matters most, try scheduling it. There are many methods, such as setting aside a daily time slot or even an entire day for strategic work, or closing your email for a while. The point is to decide in advance when you'll do the task, and then protect that block of time as if it's an important meeting you can't miss. And don't let unexpected demands interrupt it—because something will always come up.

Adapted from "How to Focus on What's Important,
Not Just What's Urgent," by Alice Boyes

Open Up—Without Oversharing

It's generally good when your employees feel a personal connection to you, but sharing too many of your thoughts and feelings can undermine your authority. Evaluate a personal comment by considering how you'd feel if your boss said it to you. For example, telling employees you're in a bad mood because you're having a lousy day is probably fine; telling them you're in a bad mood because you had a big fight with your partner this morning probably isn't. If you wouldn't mind hearing a certain comment, chances are your team will feel the same. Otherwise, err on the side of caution.

Adapted from "How Leaders Can Open Up to Their Teams Without Oversharing," by Liz Fosslien and Mollie West Duffy

To Widen Your Perspective, Imagine You're the CEO

It's easy to lose sight of how your job fits into the broader organization. Keep the bigger picture in mind by playing CEO for a day. Imagine that you hold the top job, and consider your meetings, projects, and emails from that perspective. CEOs often have to balance conflicting needs and roles to make a decision. So how would a CEO respond or react in the situation you're in? What value would the chief executive find in your assignments and activities? And, importantly, how might that perspective lead you to change something about your work?

Adapted from "What Startup Employees Can Teach the Rest of Us About Work," by Anand Chopra-McGowan

You Aren't as Good at Coaching as You Think

As a leader, you probably tend to think you're a good coach. But some leaders overestimate their skills—by a wide margin. The problem? Deep down, they've decided on a way forward before they even talk to the employee. A better approach starts with you listening to the person, asking questions, and withholding judgment. Try to draw wisdom, insight, and creativity from the employee, with the goal of helping them learn to solve problems on their own. This approach to coaching can be challenging if you're used to telling people what to do. But it's highly energizing, and more effective, for the person being coached.

Adapted from "The Leader as Coach,"
by Herminia Ibarra and Anne Scoular

You're Looking at Customers All Wrong

"The view that an industry is a customer-satisfying process, not a goods-producing process, is vital for all businesspeople to understand. An industry begins with the customer and [their] needs, not with a patent, a raw material, or a selling skill. Given the customer's needs, the industry develops backwards, first concerning itself with the physical *delivery* of customer satisfactions. Then it moves back further to *creating* the things by which these satisfactions are in part achieved. How these materials are created is a matter of indifference to the customer, hence the . . . form of manufacturing, processing, [etc.] cannot be considered . . . a vital aspect of the industry. Finally, the industry moves back still further to *finding* the raw materials necessary for making its products."

Adapted from "Marketing Myopia,"
by Theodore Levitt

Should You Stop Deliberating and Make a Decision?

Waiting to make decisions can slow down your company and lead to missed opportunities. But when do you need more data or deliberation and when should you just make a choice? Consider two factors.

- **Importance.** For less significant issues, pick something and move on. For big decisions with wide or long-term impact, reflect or gather additional information before you choose.

- **Frequency.** If the issue requiring a decision happens often, creating a system for it could help, even if it requires an initial time investment. If the issue is rare, getting a variety of perspectives before making a choice could be valuable.

Whatever you decide, reflect to learn what worked and what needs improvement next time.

Adapted from "When to Stop Deliberating and Just
Make a Decision," by Thomas H. Davenport

Reframe Regret About Paths Not Taken

Years or decades into your career, you may feel regret about the paths you didn't take. Even if you love your job in finance, the careers you didn't pursue (in fashion or literature, say) can loom large in your mind. One way to deal with this feeling is to reframe it. Regret doesn't necessarily mean something is wrong; you'd mourn unpursued futures no matter what you chose. The only way to avoid it would be to care about only one thing. So remind yourself that feeling you've missed out is the inevitable consequence of something good: your capacity to find worth in many walks of life.

Adapted from "Facing Your Mid-Career Crisis,"
by Kieran Setiya

Cross-Cultural Leadership Calls for Nuance

When advice for leading international teams relies on clichés or stereotypes—the Japanese are hierarchical, or the French favor subtle communication—the result is oversimplified and erroneous assumptions. To lead effectively across cultures, seek out a nuanced understanding of the people you're working with. Check your knee-jerk tendencies, and examine and adapt your leadership style. Getting advice from local peers can help you understand employees' expectations for areas such as giving and receiving feedback, making decisions, and building trust. Practicing a variety of leadership styles will help you motivate and mobilize team members, no matter where you are or who you're working with.

Adapted from "Navigating the Cultural Minefield,"
by Erin Meyer

What Great Questions Do

Showcase Your Expertise (Without Bragging)

A great question can help you learn more about a task, unlock hidden opportunities, deliver better results, and mitigate unforeseen risks. One mark of a great question is that it showcases your expertise without showing off. You want to prove what you bring to the table, but do it briefly and tactfully. For example, don't say, "I studied marketing at Harvard and have helped *Fortune* 500 companies modernize their marketing channels. What channels do you want to expand?" Instead, say, "I'd love to use my experience in marketing at *Fortune* 500 companies to support your growth. What does your marketing department want to expand?"

Adapted from "The Art of Asking Great Questions,"
by Tijs Besieux

Write Down Your Team's Unwritten Rules

Every workplace has unwritten rules, the cultural and emotional norms that dictate what's acceptable. But is everyone aware of them? To keep everyone on the same page, clarify uncertainties by writing them down. With your team, brainstorm an "It's OK to . . ." list. For example, the list might include "It's OK to say you don't understand a process," or, "It's OK to turn off your video during a virtual meeting," or "It's OK to go for a short walk in the middle of the day."

Documenting your norms is helpful for new, current, and future employees alike, and allows you to reinforce your team culture when circumstances change.

Adapted from "Write Down Your Team's Unwritten Rules,"
by Liz Fosslien and Mollie West Duffy

Leading People Who Know More Than You Do

No matter how great your expertise, eventually you'll be promoted to a level where your team members know more about a business problem than you do. Don't try to master a new topic overnight—expertise is built over the long term. Instead, shift your role from providing solutions to empowering your team of experts. Take a big-picture view of the business problem, ask questions about facts and assumptions, and ensure your team is framing the issue correctly. You still play a vital role even when you aren't the smartest person in the room. Be the leader your experts need.

Adapted from "Leading People When They Know More
Than You Do," by Wanda T. Wallace and David Creelman

Surviving When You Didn't Sleep Well

You know that sleep is essential to your health and performance. But what happens when you can't get enough? There are a few ways to stay productive when you slept badly. For example, focus on routine tasks that don't require creativity, which is hard to muster when you're depleted. Try to avoid more-complex work, since sleep deprivation makes you more prone to mistakes. Look for ways to rely on other people, too. For example, ask a colleague to look over your document for mistakes, and offer to return the favor later. Finally, if you can, consider a nap. Even 20 minutes of rest can recharge your effectiveness.

Adapted from "Sleep Well, Lead Better,"
by Christopher M. Barnes

Anxiety Can Make You a Better Leader

Anxiety can zap your energy and drive you to make poor decisions, but it can also help you react quickly to threats and get more comfortable with uncomfortable feelings. To start channeling your anxiety effectively, notice when it manifests and how it feels. Observe your physical reactions, such as a churning in your stomach, and your emotional ones, such as feeling overwhelmed or panicked. Keep a journal to become more aware of these reactions over time. Once you know how your anxiety feels, you can spot when it's appearing, cuing you to pause, calm yourself, and prevent the anxiety from taking over.

Adapted from "Leading Through Anxiety,"
by Morra Aarons-Mele

Have Realistic Expectations of Your Boss

A common misconception, especially from people earlier in their careers, is that your boss magically knows what information or help you need without your telling them. While some bosses are proactive and thoughtful enough to meet that expectation, it's unrealistic for the majority of managers. Much more reasonable is to remember that your boss is only human: They can't read your mind and they have a lot on their plate. So assume responsibility for your own career and development. If you need certain information or resources to do your job, don't wait for your boss to provide it—talk to them about how they can help.

Adapted from "Managing Your Boss,"
by John J. Gabarro and John P. Kotter

Gut-Check Your New Idea

New ideas are exciting. Whether you've thought of a product, a process improvement, or an expansion of the strategy, you may feel ready to charge ahead and implement it. But no one person can anticipate every potential problem, threat, or opportunity. So take the time to get perspectives from your colleagues—especially those from other departments and backgrounds. Ask them six questions:

1. What stands out to you?

2. What's missing?

3. What would our critics say?

4. What would it look like if we failed?

5. What would customer-facing employees say about our idea?

6. What shortcomings would please our competitors?

Use the responses to hone and iterate on your idea.

Adapted from "Think You Have a Great Idea? Ask These 6 Questions to Gain Perspective," by Sabina Nawaz

Being in Charge Doesn't Mean You're Completely in Control

New managers often fail, at least initially, because they have misconceptions about what it means to be a boss. One of these myths is that top-down control over your team members is the best way to lead. But no one wants to work for a controlling boss, so leading like one can backfire and reduce your power. Instead, lead with influence by holding people to high standards—but letting them seize the initiative, take calculated risks, and work in the ways they prefer. Sharing power with employees this way can actually make you *more* influential, since they'll see that you're committed to helping them succeed.

Adapted from "Becoming the Boss,"
by Linda A. Hill

Bias Doesn't Have to Be Intentional to Hold Women Back

"Bias does not require an intent to exclude; nor does it necessarily produce direct, immediate harm to any individual. Rather, it creates a context—akin to 'something in the water'—in which women fail to thrive or reach their full potential. Feeling less connected to one's male colleagues, being advised to take a staff role to accommodate family, finding oneself excluded from consideration for key positions—all these situations reflect work structures and practices that put women at a disadvantage. Without an understanding of second-generation bias, people are left with stereotypes to explain why women . . . have failed to achieve parity with men: If they can't reach the top, it is because they 'don't ask,' are 'too nice,' or simply 'opt out.'"

Adapted from "Women Rising: The Unseen Barriers,"
by Herminia Ibarra, Robin J. Ely, and Deborah M. Kolb

What's Your Leadership Style?

Affiliative

Your personal leadership style has a powerful impact on your organization. One type of leadership that has positive effects on an organization's working environment and results is the affiliative style. Affiliative leaders strive to increase morale, improve communication, and repair broken trust. They focus on building emotional bonds and offering lots of positive feedback. As a result, loyalty, risk-taking, and a sense of belonging flourish. However, this approach's focus on praise can mean poor performance goes uncorrected and employees wonder how to improve—so you must also provide clear direction and standards. As you lead, think about what style a situation calls for, and whether your current approach is working well or may need an adjustment.

Adapted from "Leadership That Gets Results,"
by Daniel Goleman

Build the Internal Network You Need

When people are promoted, 49% underperform for up to 18 months, Gartner surveys show. The problem? They don't have internal networks that help them succeed. To prepare for a leadership role, proactively build a broad, mutually beneficial network. Here's how:

- Uncover the "informal org chart," those well-connected leaders who shape opinion and help things get done.

- Learn those leaders' priorities and interests and show that you're willing to help achieve them.

- Identify how you do and don't add value, and partner with people who can fill any gaps.

- Spend time with well-connected peers. The more people you know, the more ideas and resources you'll have access to.

Adapted from "How to Succeed Quickly in a New Role,"
by Rob Cross, Greg Pryor, and David Sylvester

Great Mentors Establish a Mentorship Team

Since your time is limited, and because your knowledge and experience aren't the only things someone will need to thrive, build a team of advisers for your mentee. Think about what areas the person wants to learn about and grow in, as well as who in your network has expertise to offer. Then ask relevant peers if they're willing to help. You'll be the go-to source of moral, career, and institutional support, but the team approach ensures your mentee can always get a breadth of help when they need it. Plus, your peers may enjoy contributing to someone's growth with a lower level of commitment.

Adapted from "6 Things Every Mentor Should Do,"
by Vineet Chopra and Sanjay Saint

Questions to Ask Often

Wait, What?

When you ask great questions, you inspire curiosity, creativity, and deeper thinking in yourself and in your employees. One useful question is "Wait, what?" which can prevent someone (especially you) from jumping to conclusions or listening only to form a quick opinion. When something doesn't sound quite right or seems too easy a solution, ask colleagues and employees to slow down. "Wait, what?" is an exercise in understanding, which is critical to making informed decisions. It gives the other person a chance to explain their thinking, or to revisit their assumptions.

Adapted from "5 Questions Leaders Should Be Asking
All the Time," by James E. Ryan

Too Busy?
Buy Back Time

Not enough hours in the day? Buying back time—by spending money on services that help you get more done—is good for your happiness, stress levels, and health, according to research from Harvard Business School. You might, for example, outsource chores you dislike, such as paying to have groceries delivered or your house cleaned. You could also do less comparison shopping, since the time needed to endlessly hunt for a better price (say, for a flight or a hotel room) is probably worth more than the money you'd save. After all, you'll make more money in the future; once your time is gone, it's gone for good.

Adapted from "Time for Happiness,"
by Ashley Whillans

Transition to Senior Leadership

Become an Integrator

When you shift from leading a function to leading an enterprise, you must navigate a tricky set of changes in your leadership focus and skills. One change is becoming an integrator. As a functional leader, your job was to manage people who focus in analytical depth on specific business activities. Now, your role is to integrate the collective knowledge of functional teams to solve organizational problems. The key skills you need are understanding competing issues, knowing how to make trade-offs, and explaining the rationale for those decisions. But there's no substitute for actually making the calls and learning from their outcome.

Adapted from "How Managers Become Leaders,"
by Michael D. Watkins

What Successful People Do

Track Progress and Practice Realistic Optimism

Why have you been so successful in reaching some of your goals, but not others? Even brilliant, highly accomplished people aren't great at understanding why they succeed or fail. But successful people do a few things differently, according to decades of research on achievement. One is monitoring your progress toward your goals. If you don't know how you're doing, you can't adjust accordingly. So check your progress frequently—weekly, or even daily. Don't overestimate your accomplishments or underestimate how difficult it will be to meet your goal. Positive thinking is great, but successful people are realistic optimists. Plan ahead to put in the time, effort, and persistence you'll need to accomplish your goals.

Adapted from "Nine Things Successful People
Do Differently," by Heidi Grant

Make Creativity Predictable

Creativity doesn't have to depend on a flash of inspiration—you can create the conditions for it. Here are some tactics:

- Spend time considering the problem you're trying to solve—and then walk away from it. Give your brain a chance to draw connections and sort through possible paths forward.

- Expand your interests. Follow your curiosity. Read an article on a topic that intrigues you. Watch a webinar on a subject that seems irrelevant to your work but tickles your brain. You never know what dots you may connect when you have built a rich mental database to draw from.

- When inspiration hits, stop what you're doing and get to work. Don't let those moments go by without capturing your ideas on paper.

Adapted from "How to Be Creative on Demand,"
by Joseph Grenny

How to Make Your Employees Quit

Waste Resources

Losing an employee hurts morale and productivity, and replacing people who leave is expensive. One mistake that can lead your people to quit is wasting resources. If your team doesn't have what they need to succeed, they're set up to fail. Time is one resource that gets wasted often, especially in endless meetings. Help your team prioritize their highest-importance, highest-impact work, and support them in guarding the time they need to do it. Before assigning someone more work or inviting them to another meeting, stop and consider whether this person is the only one who could take it on. If not, find someone else.

Adapted from "8 Things Leaders Do That Make
Employees Quit," by Jon Christiansen

Don't Be a Victim of Your Success

Learn to Say "I Don't Know"

To keep performing at your best, you must overcome the barriers that accompany your success. One barrier is thinking you know it all. The higher you rise in the corporate ranks, the easier it is to believe that you already know everything you need to. And the harder it can get to say an essential phrase that many leaders struggle with: "I don't know." But unless you can admit you don't have all the answers, it's hard to tackle the complex, ambiguous problems that senior leaders encounter.

Do you ever struggle to say "I don't know"? Why?

Adapted from "Want to Change the World? Don't Let Your Own Success Get in the Way," by Rosabeth Moss Kanter

Promote Inclusive Language in Your Organization

Business vocabulary is littered with terms that exclude people. To create a truly inclusive culture, take a hard look at how people in your company use language. For example, make sure job descriptions don't use terms like "hacker" or "ninja," which may deter people of color, women, people with disabilities, or older job candidates; alternatives like "programmer" or "software engineer" are neutral and clearer. To help, you may want to create—and then share—a company guide to inclusive language. It should outline practical, accessible tips and tools that employees can use, and make sure people across the company can contribute input to it.

Adapted from "How to Make Your Organization's Language More Inclusive," by Odessa S. Hamilton, Lindsay Kohler, Elle Bradley Cox, and Grace Lordan

How Does Authenticity Shape Your Leadership?

As an authentic leader, you practice your values and stay true to who you are. That consistency helps you build strong relationships and inspire your team. There's no one way to be authentic, but a few questions can help you reflect on what it means to you: Where do your most deeply held values come from? Which people and experiences in your early life had the greatest impact on you? What is your core self—when you say, "This is the real me"—at work and at home? What motivates you, both extrinsically and intrinsically? Who's on your support team, and how do they help you focus on what matters most?

Adapted from "Discovering Your Authentic Leadership," by Bill George, Peter Sims, Andrew N. McLean, and Diana Mayer

Storytelling to Drive Change

Honor the Past

When your organization needs to make a big change, stories can help you convey not only why it needs to transform but also what the future will look like in specific, vivid terms. Good storytelling does four things. One of them is honoring the past. To get everyone on board with your ideas, show that you intend to preserve what's best about the company. In addition, you must confront the organization's history with both optimism and honesty—which includes acknowledging the human cost of past mistakes. Showing that you know what needs to change, and what should stay the same, will help you win people over.

Adapted from "Storytelling That Drives Bold Change,"
by Frances X. Frei and Anne Morriss

Know Your Emotional Impact

As a leader, your mood has a huge impact on the performance of others. But leaders often don't realize how their moods and actions appear to others. Why? People don't tell you the whole truth about your emotional impact. Maybe they're scared to be the bearer of bad news. Or they think it isn't their place to say something. Perhaps they don't realize that what they really want to talk about is the effect of your emotional style. Whatever the reason, you can't rely on people to spontaneously give you the full picture.

How can you make sure you're getting the crucial feedback you need about your emotional impact?

Adapted from "Primal Leadership: The Hidden Driver
of Great Performance," by Daniel Goleman,
Richard E. Boyatzis, and Annie McKee

When Your Team's Vibe Is Off

Rethink Its Communication Habits

If your team is feeling stuck or stale, it could be because employees have lost sight of their purpose and the goals they're working toward. Whether the malaise is due to external factors or internal ones (or both), sometimes your team's communication habits need a refresh. Discussing a few questions as a group can help:

1. What channels can we use more effectively?

2. What information needs to be shared synchronously, and what can be shared asynchronously?

3. How can we reduce distractions to help each other focus more?

Use the answers to improve how your team communicates, from meetings to email to messaging tools. You should also rethink your norms around those methods, including expected response times for email and how often people need to check messaging tools.

Adapted from "20 Questions to Ask When Your
Team's Vibe Is Off," by Liane Davey

Leading Through Uncertainty

Practice Caring Transparency

When the world feels uncertain and chaotic, you have no clue what will happen next. How can you reassure employees and help them stay focused? One way to lead well in these conditions is to be transparently caring. That means being honest about what's on your mind and in your heart, especially when you need to make unpopular but necessary decisions. Don't hold back important information because of how it will be received; tell people what's happening and where they stand—and do so clearly and compassionately. Being candid with employees shows that you care about them.

Adapted from "3 Strategies for Leading Through Difficult Times,"
by Rasmus Hougaard, Jacqueline Carter, and Rob Stembridge

Good Leaders Offer a Dissenting Opinion

"Being a leader also means being willing to speak up, even when you're expressing an unpopular view. CEOs' proposals often generate head nodding, even from people who secretly harbor serious reservations. In reality, most [leaders] desperately want dissenting opinions so they can make better choices. While emerging leaders must use good judgment regarding the tone and timing of their dissent, they also need to be aware that they can hit a plateau by playing it safe when they should be asserting their heartfelt opinions."

Adapted from "Reaching Your Potential,"
by Robert Steven Kaplan

Let Your Team Struggle

To grow and reach their full potential, your employees have to take on work they're not quite ready for; sometimes they need to struggle. And when you see that happening, you may feel tempted to step in and help; instead, let yourself and the employee both push through the discomfort. One of the keys to engaging employees is giving them hard, stimulating challenges—and they won't learn anything if you leap to their aid. So allow them to work through the challenge on their own and offer advice and support when needed. The result will be growth for both of you.

Adapted from "To Help Your Team Grow,
Give Them Space to Struggle," by Kelli Thompson

Your Leadership Voice

Built on Context

Cultivating your leadership voice requires building the capacity to respond authentically, constructively, and effectively, no matter the situation or audience. One aspect of your voice is context. As you take on senior roles, your view and perspective of the business grow—and part of the job becomes finding ways to communicate that broader context to others. Whether you're talking to employees about strategy, presenting new ideas to executives, or explaining your decision-making criteria to your team, don't dive into the details without first addressing the bigger picture of the topic at hand.

How do you use your understanding of context to help others?

———————————

Adapted from "You Don't Just Need One Leadership
Voice—You Need Many," by Amy Jen Su

Build Skills That AI Can't Copy

Embrace Analog

AI tools may compete with the lower and middle ends of many professions, such as copywriting and design. So it's critical to develop yourself in ways that AI can't copy. One way is to embrace analog and prioritize the in-person interactions that AI can't replicate. AI can only connect information it already knows—it can't produce knowledge. You, though, can find new ideas and insights by sharing meals with colleagues, attending in-person conferences, and networking with peers. Tapping into new expertise through your lived experience and personal connections is one way to give yourself an edge.

Adapted from "5 Ways to Future-Proof Your Career in the Age of AI,"
by Dorie Clark and Tomas Chamorro-Premuzic

The Character of Great Leaders

"While seemingly amorphous, character and leadership often make the difference between good performance and great performance. . . . Excellent leaders are willing to do things for others without regard to what's in it for them. They coach and mentor. They have the mindset of an owner and figure out what they would do if they were the ultimate decision-maker. They're willing to make a recommendation that would benefit the organization's overall performance, possibly to the detriment of their own unit. They have the courage to trust that they will eventually be rewarded, even if their actions may not be in their own short-term interest."

Adapted from "Reaching Your Potential,"
by Robert Steven Kaplan

"Just This Once" Thinking Will Lead You Astray

Plenty of disasters—both professional and personal—have started with "just this once" thinking. Just this once you'll fudge the numbers. Just this once you'll look the other way. Just this once you'll lie to someone. The cost of doing something wrong one time always seems alluringly low, making it easy to ignore where that path can lead. The antidote is to know what you stand for and where to draw your personal lines of what's right and what's not. Sticking to your principles 100% of the time is far easier than doing it 98% of the time.

———————

Adapted from "How Will You Measure Your Life?,"
by Clayton M. Christensen

Your Writing Could Be Clearer

Writing clearly is hard, especially when time is short. To ensure your message is coming across, follow three tips:

- **Get to the point.** Lead with your core idea, give detail to contextualize it, and cut anything extraneous.

- **Use topic sentences that tell the reader what's coming.** Go beyond details and descriptions ("I met with the client in Berlin"). Use your first sentence to introduce what the paragraph is about ("My meeting with the Berlin client focused on plans for future growth").

- **Use the active voice to explain who did what.** "Juan improved the project's results" is clearer than "The project's results were improved."

Adapted from "3 Ways to Make Your Writing Clearer," by Jane Rosenzweig

Are You Ready to Be a Manager?

There's more to becoming a leader than just being promoted. You also need to figure out your weak spots and what you don't know yet, so you can fill those gaps. Ask yourself six questions:

1. What's my leadership style?

2. How will I help my employees develop?

3. How will I prioritize and delegate work?

4. How will I deliver constructive feedback?

5. How will I resolve conflict?

6. Am I a good public speaker, and can I lead meetings effectively?

Use your answers to consider your strengths, traits, expertise, and knowledge, as well as your areas for improvement.

Adapted from "Are You Ready to Become a Manager?," by Octavia Goredema

Leaders Need a Strategic Intent

When it comes to strategy, some companies focus on trimming their ambitions to match their resources. As a result, they search only for advantages they can sustain. A better approach is to accelerate the pace of organizational learning and try to attain seemingly impossible goals. You'll need to foster the desire to succeed among your employees and maintain it by spreading the vision of global leadership. You'll also need stretch targets, which force your company to compete in innovative ways. The name for all this is *strategic intent*, and it's one way you can lead your organization beyond the competition.

What strategic intent can you set for your company?

Adapted from "Strategic Intent,"
by Gary Hamel and C.K. Prahalad

Diagnose Your Team's Lack of Accountability

If your team lacks accountability, it may be due to an underlying issue such as uncertain roles, limited resources, or a poor strategy. Diagnose the problem by considering whether you're contributing to it. Have you been clear about expectations, processes, and action plans? Hold a meeting to listen and ask questions. Gently summarize what's been happening (say, missed deadlines), and ask for employees' honest thoughts about the causes. Don't judge or offer critical feedback—be open to their perspectives. Once the true problems are clear, discuss how to help everyone get back on track, including new strategies or processes that may be needed.

Adapted from "Does Your Team Have an Accountability Problem?," by Melissa Raffoni

To Be a Better Leader, Get a Protégé

Sponsoring relationships don't just help the less-experienced person. A good protégé expands your worldview and helps you fill gaps in your skill set and knowledge, which can lead to promotions and stretch assignments. Cultivate this type of sponsoring relationship by seeking out a high-performing, trustworthy protégé. This person's reputation will become intertwined with yours, so consider how their actions may reflect on you. Protégés don't have to be young, but they should be different from you, perhaps in gender, ethnicity, professional background, or life experience. Think about what areas you want to learn about, as well as where your expertise is, and use those factors in choosing a protégé.

Adapted from "Want to Be a Better Manager? Get
a Protégé," by Sylvia Ann Hewlett

Learning to Learn

Take a Breath

Acquiring new knowledge quickly and continually is a skill that will never be obsolete. One way to do it is to be honest about your areas for improvement. We often react to negative feedback by being defensive, which is why a comment like "You need to get better at developing your employees" might produce the response "My team is fine!" When you catch yourself thinking that way, stop and consider how accurate the feedback is—and how you know. Reflecting will help you separate knee-jerk reactions from the facts, and then you can decide how to move forward productively.

Adapted from "Learning to Learn,"
by Erika Andersen

To Help Women Get Ahead

Rethink Your Hiring Process

As a leader, you know that women are still dramatically under-represented in positions of power: Few *Fortune* 500 companies are led by women, and even fewer by women of color. One way to reduce the barriers holding women back is to rethink your hiring practices, which can easily become gender biased. It's all too common for managers to assess men and women differently even when they're equally qualified for a role. Watch, too, for bias against mothers, women of childbearing age, or women in general. Having diversity on your hiring team can help, as can focusing the hiring process specifically on job criteria and using blind auditions and anonymized résumés.

Adapted from "How to Close the Gender Gap,"
by Colleen Ammerman and Boris Groysberg

Did Tough Feedback Catch You Off Guard?

When feedback is unexpectedly critical, your first instinct may be to run and hide. Four steps can help you stay present and react productively:

1. **Collect yourself.** Breathe deeply and notice your feelings. Labeling them ("I'm feeling hurt and ashamed") can help you get distance from them.

2. **Understand.** Ask the person for examples of the behavior they've highlighted. Stay calm and listen.

3. **Recover.** Tell the person that you need to reflect. Don't agree or disagree with what you've heard. Take some time to process and evaluate it.

4. **Engage.** Consider what you do and don't agree with. If necessary, talk to the person again and share your thoughts.

Adapted from "How to Be Resilient in the Face of Harsh Criticism," by Joseph Grenny

How to Lose Well

Rethink Winning and Losing

As a leader, you're focused on winning. But no one is successful all the time; you need to learn to lose with grace. One approach is to reflect on why you do what you do. If you enjoy your work and have a purpose you're pursuing, you'll care less about who "wins" and who "loses." Think of it this way: Work is finite. Projects end, companies fold, people quit. But the reason you invest so much of yourself in these ventures—your personal and professional *why*—is infinite. It never ends. So let go of the fact that things didn't go your way. Do the work because you love it.

Adapted from "Good Leaders Lose with Grace,"
by Tim Leberecht

Strategic Alignment Doesn't Just Happen

Assuming that all employees share your understanding of the company's strategy is a dangerous mistake. If you and other leaders aren't on the same page with the people implementing the strategy, different groups are likely pursuing divergent and even clashing goals. The result: politics, infighting, unproductive meetings, and serious obstacles to creating value.

What steps could you take to ensure your employees are strategically aligned?

Adapted from "Is Your Company as Strategically Aligned as You Think It Is?," by Vikas Mittal, Alessandro Piazza, and Ashwin Malshe

Ask Questions That Inspire

To be a great leader, ask powerful, inspiring questions that push people to think beyond what they've done in the past. Admit that you don't have all the answers, and bring people together to find them. For example, rather than asking, "How can we improve customer response times by 10%?" you could ask, "What unmet customer needs could be the basis of an entirely new business?" Big, broad questions show your ambition to help the company grow, while inviting employees to join you in setting and achieving new goals. They also demonstrate that questioning is important and contributes to a culture of learning.

Adapted from "Good Leadership Is About Asking Good Questions," by John Hagel III

Self-Regulation Is Key to Your Leadership

When you are in control of your feelings and impulses you create an environment of trust and fairness, so self-regulation is a critical skill for leaders. In that kind of setting, politics, turnover, and infighting are reduced and productivity is increased. But self-regulation is also important for competitive reasons. People who have mastered their emotions are able to roll with the changes, big and small, that happen in any career. If you don't see yourself in these characteristics, look for ways to improve your self-regulation. Consider how you can better control bad moods and emotional impulses when they arise, and even channel them in useful ways.

Adapted from "What Makes a Leader?,"
by Daniel Goleman

Focus on What's Important, Not on What's Urgent

Incremental Progress

Your to-do list has both important and urgent tasks. It's easy to work on what's due soonest, but sometimes the important projects need your attention more. To prioritize what matters most, focus on making incremental progress. Big projects are often composed of small tasks, so when you're setting goals, also set half-size versions. It might feel ideal to get everything done at once, but maybe it's more realistic to do half (or one-quarter, or one-tenth) of the work now. Divide up the project into chunks that feel attainable, then work to make progress on them.

———

Adapted from "How to Focus on What's Important,
Not Just What's Urgent," by Alice Boyes

Tap Your Internal Experts

Every company has people who are well-versed in key areas or serve as the firm's institutional memory. How do you ensure that they pass their insights on to their colleagues? Try a "knowledge cascade." Here's how it works. Ask the specialists in your department to share their expertise with a few people, who will then be responsible for teaching others. This knowledge cascade could happen directly, through teaching or mentoring, or in meetings where the expert presents lessons and leads discussions. Other options can work too, such as having the specialist record a podcast or video, or write something brief to explain a topic. Creating a formal process will preserve essential information.

Adapted from "How Your Organization's Experts Can Share Their Knowledge," by Dorothy Leonard and James Martin

You Need Three Types of Curiosity

Curiosity helps foster a culture of adaptability, engagement, and high performance on your team. There are three types of curiosity to cultivate:

- **Curiosity about employees.** Organizations are a collection of employees' mindsets, attitudes, and values. To understand your team better, talk to employees directly, formally survey them, or use small focus groups to learn what people care about.

- **Curiosity about yourself.** Reflect on your role and how you've evolved over time. The more you understand your trajectory, the better you'll be able to adapt to the company's future.

- **Curiosity about the organization.** Notice changes to the organization's culture, mission, vision, and values. Your company isn't static, so your understanding of it shouldn't be either.

Adapted from "Leaders, Make Curiosity the Core of Your Organizational Culture," by John Coleman

To Move On from Change

Tie the Past and Present Together

Sometimes a big change—personal or professional—upends your identity. Crafting a narrative that clearly links your history with your new future can help you move forward. Think about your goals and priorities, and how the new path forward helps you pursue them, even in unexpected ways. For example, maybe you left a high-paying career to care for an aging parent. Your narrative might highlight the fact that supporting family is important to you; you used to contribute more through salary and benefits, and now you're giving more in terms of time. These kinds of narratives can help you make peace with your transition and leave behind your old identity.

Adapted from "When a Major Life Change Upends Your Sense of Self," by Madeline Toubiana, Trish Ruebottom, and Luciana Turchick Hakak

Develop Your Learning Agility

Experiment with New Approaches

If you rely on the same assumptions and behavioral repertoires you've used for years as a leader, you are prone to stagnate, underperform, or derail, according to research from Korn Ferry. The solution is to develop learning agility, the capacity for rapid, continuous learning. One method is to experiment with your usual approaches to solving problems. Think about a challenge you're facing and how you're inclined to tackle it. Then think about other potential solutions and methods that could work. Try to view the situation from a fresh point of view, and let go of the assumption that you have to handle things the way you've always done. Free yourself to be creative; you may just discover a new approach.

Adapted from "4 Ways to Become a Better Learner,"
by Monique Valcour

Focus on Purpose, Not Perception

"Women are taught to downplay femininity, or to soften a hard-charging style, or to try to strike a perfect balance between the two. But the time and energy spent on managing these perceptions can ultimately be self-defeating. Anchoring in purpose enables women to redirect their attention toward shared goals and to consider who they need to be and what they need to learn in order to achieve those goals. Instead of defining themselves in relation to gender stereotypes—whether rejecting stereotypically masculine approaches because they feel inauthentic or rejecting stereotypically feminine ones for fear that they convey incompetence—female leaders can focus on behaving in ways that advance the purposes for which they stand."

Adapted from "Women Rising: The Unseen Barriers,"
by Herminia Ibarra, Robin J. Ely, and Deborah M. Kolb

Break Your Career-Limiting Habit

Spend Time with New People

We all have a career-limiting habit, such as procrastinating or using our phones when we should be connecting with others. But people who overcome bad habits take control of the circumstances that feed them, according to research from Crucial Learning. One way to do this is to spend more time with people who help build the behaviors you need to cultivate. For example, if you want to have a better attitude about company changes, interact more with those who support the changes, and spend less time with people who oppose them. Our friends and colleagues help shape how we think and feel, so thoughtfully use that fact to your advantage.

Adapted from "Trick Yourself into Breaking a
Bad Habit," by Joseph Grenny

Focus DEI Efforts on Systems, Not People

DEI initiatives can cause backlash because they feel like a judgment of employees' inherent skills, competence, and goodness. That's why you should frame your DEI efforts as changing systems, not people. Start by diagnosing specific inequities in your organization. Use a mix of quantitative and qualitative data—surveys, focus groups, HR metrics—and employee demographic data to identify unequal aspects of the employee experience. Aim to understand not only what inequities exist, but also why and how they came about. Next, present a case for change to decision-makers—emphasizing that systems, policies, and practices need fixing, not employees. If you avoid blaming or shaming individuals or groups, you'll have a better chance of success.

Adapted from "To Avoid DEI Backlash, Focus on Changing Systems—Not People," by Lily Zheng

Responding to an Ultimatum in a Negotiation

Many people use ultimatums to elicit concessions from the other party. What should you do if you're on the receiving end? One tactic is to adopt a *choice mindset*, which helps you see multiple options. Before the negotiation, make a list of all the options that you and your counterpart might have. Think broadly. Then use the list if the negotiation stalls. For example, if you're interviewing for a new job and the company won't budge on salary, pivot to discussing the number of vacation days or amount of travel you'd take on. When you understand all the choices available to you, you're less likely to cave in.

Adapted from "How to Respond to 'Take It or Leave It,'"
by Anyi Ma, Yu Yang, and Krishna Savani

When Leading Your Former Peers, Listen Before You Act

When you become the boss, you'll need to establish a new reputation so that your former peers see you as leader. You probably have lots of ideas you want to implement—but wait. Before you make big changes, build your credibility by meeting with people both as a team and individually to discuss your vision for the group. Listen as much as you talk; your goal should be to explain how you will lead and also to ask how you can help your new direct reports succeed. Once you get their buy-in, you'll be better positioned to enact the strategy and direction you want.

Adapted from "How to Manage Your Former Peers,"
by Amy Gallo

When Your Team's Vibe Is Off

Rethink Its Dynamics

If your team is feeling stuck or stale, it could be because employees have lost sight of their purpose and the goals they're working toward. Whether the malaise is due to external factors or internal ones (or both), sometimes your team's dynamics need a refresh. Discussing a few questions as a group can help:

1. What norms or expectations do we need to establish or revise?

2. How can we resolve conflicts better?

3. What team activities could improve trust and candor?

Use these questions to identify issues that are holding the team back, then discuss experimenting with alternative ways of working. Revisit the questions periodically, since your team dynamic will evolve as people come and go, and as circumstances change.

Adapted from "20 Questions to Ask When Your Team's
Vibe Is Off," by Liane Davey

Tips for When Work Gets Hectic

To cope with intense times at work, try a few approaches to see what helps. One is to reward yourself for finishing a tough task (like writing a report) by completing an easy task (like running an errand). This will give your brain a break while you stay productive. Another tactic is to motivate yourself with the pleasurable parts of hard projects. If you don't love researching and verifying data, let yourself look forward to designing and delivering a clear and engaging presentation. A third approach is to use scraps of time for mental rest. Whether it's before a meeting or in line at the grocery store, breathe deeply, drop your shoulders, and unwind.

Adapted from "How to Get Through an Extremely Busy Time at Work," by Alice Boyes

Invite Input from Everyone

One way to build psychological safety on your team is to cultivate an environment where everyone can express their ideas and
concerns. Actively invite team members to give you their input.
Some people get nervous about sharing their bold ideas and con-
trary opinions, so don't assume all employees will tell you what
they're thinking, or that they always know you want to hear from
them. Explicitly ask open-ended questions like "What do you
really think about this?" and "Where do you stand on this topic?"
Show your team that you want them to question assumptions
and push back on flawed thinking—including yours.

Adapted from "What Is Psychological Safety?,"
by Amy Gallo

Are You Teaching Your Employees Enough?

"Star managers emphasize ongoing, intensive one-on-one tutoring of their direct reports, either in person or virtually, in the course of daily work. . . . The exceptional leaders I studied were teachers through and through. They routinely spent time in the trenches with employees, passing on technical skills, general tactics, business principles, and life lessons. Their teaching was informal and organic, flowing out of the tasks at hand. And it had an unmistakable impact: Their teams and organizations were some of the highest performing in their sectors."

Adapted from "The Best Leaders Are Great Teachers,"
by Sydney Finkelstein

Storytelling to Drive Change

Describe the Way Forward

When your organization needs to make a big change, stories can help you convey not only why it needs to transform but also what the future will look like in specific, vivid terms. Good storytelling does four things. One of them is describing a rigorous, optimistic way forward. Get into the weeds of your plan: What persuaded you to choose the road ahead? How confident are you about it? Data can help with rigor; use a few (only a few) data points as plot points in your story. For optimism, show why you're enthusiastic about the plan. Optimism is contagious, and you'll need it to convert stakeholders to your vision.

Adapted from "Storytelling That Drives Bold Change,"
by Frances X. Frei and Anne Morriss

Find Daily Opportunities to Mentor Employees

Your company may have a formal mentoring program, but that isn't always enough to fully engage everyone. To help all employees thrive, look for development opportunities in daily interactions. Check in by asking how things are going and offering resources and support. Learn people's priorities with questions like "What are your career goals, and how can I help?" And when you observe employees in action, offer to provide feedback about what they did well and how they could do even better next time. Informal mentoring like this can boost retention, loyalty, and commitment.

Adapted from "Real Mentorship Starts with Company Culture, Not Formal Programs," by W. Brad Johnson and David G. Smith

Get Your Hybrid Presentation Right

When you're presenting to both in-person and remote audiences, don't neglect the latter group's needs. Ask virtual participants to keep their cameras on, and alternate looking at the in-person crowd and directly at your camera, to engage everyone. If you're standing away from your laptop, occasionally move toward the camera to keep virtual participants connected to you. Continue addressing them throughout; it's too easy to focus solely on those in the room. If your presentation involves breakout groups, mix in-person and remote people together, to treat everyone equally. Finally, keep your talk short—every presentation feels longer when you're the one staring at a screen.

Adapted from "How to Nail a Hybrid Presentation,"
by Sarah Gershman and Rae Ringel

Transition to Senior Leadership

Become a Strategist

When you shift from leading a function to leading an enterprise, you must navigate a tricky set of changes in your leadership focus and skills. One change is becoming a strategist. The immediate, concrete results of being tactical are seductive. But your job now is to be strategist-in-chief. You need three skills: shifting between details and the big picture, recognizing patterns in complex environments, and anticipating how outside parties (say, competitors or the media) will respond to what you do. Strategic thinking can be improved with training, so seek out opportunities in the company to strengthen your own.

Adapted from "How Managers Become Leaders,"
by Michael D. Watkins

Questions to Ask Yourself

Do I Give Effective Feedback?

Through the ups and downs of your career, regularly asking yourself a few questions can help you stay on track with your goals and priorities. One of those questions is: Do you give timely, direct, constructive feedback? Your team wants to know how to grow and develop, but they need you to help them do it. Don't wait for end-of-year reviews; giving feedback more often equips people to make improvements now rather than in the future. It also shows you're invested in their success, which increases trust in the relationship.

How are you building a culture where you're supporting your team's performance?

Adapted from "What to Ask the Person in the Mirror,"
by Robert Steven Kaplan

Think Growth Opportunities, Not Industries

"There is no such thing as a growth industry. . . . There are only companies organized and operated to create and capitalize on growth opportunities. Industries that assume themselves to be riding some automatic growth escalator invariably descend into stagnation. The history of every dead and dying 'growth' industry shows a self-deceiving cycle of bountiful expansion and undetected decay. There are four conditions that usually guarantee this cycle:

1. The belief that growth is assured by an expanding and more affluent population

2. The belief that there is no competitive substitute for the industry's major product

3. Too much faith in mass production and in the advantages of rapidly declining unit costs as output rises

4. Preoccupation with a product that lends itself to carefully controlled scientific experimentation, improvement, and manufacturing cost reduction."

Adapted from "Marketing Myopia," by Theodore Levitt

Develop a Strategy for Your Career

Take Inventory

To ensure a meaningful career, create a long-term strategy for it. One step is to take inventory of how much "career fuel" you have. That is, do you have enough transportable skills, meaningful experiences, and enduring relationships—the things that sustain you through your working years?

Assess whether your fuel levels are growing, stagnating, or even declining, and consider what you can do to replenish them. You don't always need to change jobs or industries to add fuel. Look for new pathways within your own organization through a special assignment, job rotation, expanded responsibilities, or structured training.

Adapted from "Developing a Strategy for a Life of Meaningful Labor," by Brian Fetherstonhaugh

Strengthen Your Focus

Being a focused leader doesn't mean concentrating on the three most important priorities of the year, or being the most brilliant systems thinker, or being the most in tune with your corporate culture. You are a focused leader when you command the full range of your attention: You're in touch with your inner feelings, you can control your impulses, you're aware of how others see you, you understand what others need from you, you can weed out distractions and also allow your mind to roam widely. None of that is easy—but practically every form of focus can be strengthened. What it takes is a willingness to exercise your attention like a muscle.

How can you exercise your own attention better?

Adapted from "The Focused Leader,"
by Daniel Goleman

Make Your Data Relatable

To help people wrap their heads around your data points, compare them with something concrete and relatable. For a time span or length, use something people can imagine, such as a common flight ("Imagine flying from New York to London three times"). For a size, use a familiar place, such as a local sports arena ("Imagine filling the soccer stadium five times"). And since different audiences have different frames of reference, adapt your references to their city or country ("Imagine flying from Tokyo to Singapore six times"). These kinds of comparisons help people contextualize the numbers and avoid getting lost in them.

Adapted from "3 Ways to Help People Understand What
Your Data Means," by Nancy Duarte

What You Say and Do Matters

What makes people feel included in organizations? What leaders say and do, finds research from UNSW Business School and Deloitte Australia. Whether you're already a leader or you aspire to be one, this matters because the more people feel included, the more they will speak up, go the extra mile, and collaborate. To become a more inclusive leader, try showing humility about your shortcomings, getting granular feedback on your everyday behaviors that support or inhibit people, and putting yourself in new and uncomfortable situations to expand your horizons. These behaviors aren't just critical for your personal development—they encourage employees to commit to their own growth too.

Adapted from "The Key to Inclusive Leadership,"
by Juliet Bourke and Andrea Titus

How to Make Your Employees Quit

Misassign Roles

Losing an employee hurts morale and productivity, and replacing people who leave is expensive. One mistake that can lead your people to quit is putting them in the wrong roles. If employees aren't using their full talents and knowledge, they can feel undervalued and invisible. When you identify gaps between their job and their abilities, talk about them with your employee and discuss which of their tasks are the best use of their time. Then look for ways to help them take on bigger responsibilities. Ask your employee about their career goals, which will help you consider what kinds of new tasks will help them get to where they want to go.

Adapted from "8 Things Leaders Do That Make
Employees Quit," by Jon Christiansen

Successful Leaders Contribute in Multiple Dimensions

"I think about leaders' contribution to a company along three dimensions. The first, which I call 'vertical differentiation,' is the most familiar: Some are smarter or more strategic or more knowledgeable or more charismatic. . . . CEOs are also horizontally differentiated, by which I mean they possess a variety of different skills and knowledge and leadership styles, which fit better or worse in a particular industry or situation. . . . Finally, there is the additional complication that the value a CEO adds is not just a function of what they do individually, but the extent to which they are able to influence what *other* people in the company do. Successful CEOs influence and motivate their teams, and that is essentially a social skill, not a question of vision or intelligence."

Adapted from "The Myth of the Brilliant, Charismatic Leader," by Raffaella Sadun

Don't Let Perfectionism Derail You

Use a Checklist

Perfectionism can push you to deliver excellent work, but it can also increase your anxiety and lower your productivity. To corral your perfectionism, learn when it's time to let go and move on. One tactic is to create a checklist of a task's essentials. If you're working on a client pitch, for example, the list could include ensuring that your presentation addresses the client's major concerns and details why the client should hire your company. Your inner perfectionist might fret over the font choice and every semicolon—but once the checklist is complete, take a breath and slowly back away.

Adapted from "How to Manage Your Perfectionism,"
by Rebecca Knight

164

Having Difficult Conversations—Virtually

When difficult conversations can't happen face-to-face, take a few steps to help them go smoothly. Don't use email or instant messages, since you'll lose emotional nuance with them. Instead, use a video call (not just audio) so that eye contact, facial expressions, and tone of voice are more apparent. Aim to help the other person understand both what you're saying and how you're saying it. During the conversation, be specific and detailed. When we're physically distant from someone, we're more likely to view them, or the difficult situation, abstractly. Making notes before the meeting can ensure that you cover all the points you need to.

Adapted from "How to Have Difficult Conversations
Virtually," by Art Markman

Don't Let Your Expertise Hold You Back

It's great to have deep knowledge, but if you believe your usual methods are the best—or only—way to get things done, you'll miss out on new ideas, fail to anticipate trends, and narrow your perspective. To avoid this trap, commit to constant learning and growth. Check your ego by seeking out fresh ideas and revisiting your assumptions. Surround yourself with people who don't look and think like you. Encourage colleagues at different career stages to share topics they're excited about and point out insights you might have missed. Regularly reflect on what you've learned from teammates. Learning—just like building your expertise—is a lifelong pursuit.

Adapted from "Don't Be Blinded by Your Own Expertise,"
by Sydney Finkelstein

Commit to Practicing Mindfulness

You know the benefits of practicing mindfulness—less stress and better self-control, among many others—but sustaining the habit over time isn't easy. Make mindfulness a part of your routine by structuring it. To start, schedule it at a nonnegotiable time, such as 20 minutes right after lunch. Block off the time on your calendar and consider telling your team members about it so they won't interrupt. Another tactic is to join a mindfulness group, which provides both accountability and a set time to practice. By creating a structure for mindfulness, you'll have an easier time sticking with it.

Adapted from "Make Mindfulness a Habit,"
by Matthias Birk

How Do You Perform Best?

Your performance is unique to you; understanding your style will help you produce your best work. Ask yourself a few questions to figure it out: Do you take in information by reading or listening? Do you learn by writing things down, talking through ideas, seeing something demonstrated, or trying it yourself? Do you prefer to work alone or with others? Do you produce results by making decisions or advising decision-makers? Do you perform well under stress or need structure and predictability? Do you work best in a big company or a small one? It's worth reflecting on these questions occasionally, since they can evolve given your current context.

Adapted from "Managing Oneself,"
by Peter F. Drucker

Build Your Collaboration Skills

External Self-Awareness

Teams are interconnected systems of preferences, skills, experiences, and perspectives. To lead such a complex entity well, you must develop your *external* self-awareness. Doing so involves reflecting on how your words and actions impact others; without that foundational understanding, you'll struggle to make the best possible contributions.

To build your external self-awareness, observe how others react to you in discussions: Did someone raise their voice? Stop talking? Lean back in their chair? Consider what various reactions may indicate about your communication and style. Ask trusted colleagues about behaviors you have that are helpful and unhelpful. Getting this kind of feedback will make you more attuned to those you lead.

Adapted from "To Improve Your Team, First Work on Yourself," by Jennifer Porter

Maintaining Psychological Safety

Spot—and Stop—Bad Behavior

When we perceive others to be a threat, we're less likely to listen effectively, ask questions, or share our ideas. That's one reason why maintaining psychological safety on your team is so important. One way to build (or rebuild) it is to have zero tolerance for bad behavior. If you witness someone engaging in blatant rudeness—such as dismissing, steamrolling, or using derogatory language—address it immediately. Take the person aside, explain why their behavior is unacceptable, and be specific about how they need to change. By holding everyone accountable for their actions, you'll show that the same standards apply to all.

Adapted from "Do You Really Trust Your Team?
(And Do They Trust You?)," by Amy Jen Su

What Messages Is Your Calendar Sending?

Your schedule is a symbol of how you lead and what's important to you. The way you allocate your time and presence—the tasks and people you show up for—shows the rest of the organization what you care about. It can also affect your legitimacy if you spend too little time on important things or too much on less trivial ones. And the higher you rise in the company, the stronger these dynamics become.

What messages does your schedule communicate about your priorities? What adjustments could you make to better align them?

Adapted from "How CEOs Manage Time,"
by Michael E. Porter and Nitin Nohria

Fight a Toxic Company Culture with a Healthy Team Culture

If your company's culture has toxic norms that drag down your employees' behavior, create a microculture for your team of healthy, positive behaviors. Think about your values. Hold a meeting, or several meetings, for team members to discuss what's important to them and what they want and need from each other. Articulate the team's shared values and the rules of engagement that will guide everyone's behavior going forward. Once the group reaches agreement, codify the new norms in a team code of conduct. You may not be able to change your company's culture, but you can change your team's.

Adapted from "Keep Your Company's Toxic Culture from Infecting Your Team," by Annie McKee

Great Mentors Run a Tight Ship

Make your mentoring relationship more efficient by establishing ground rules up front. Start by asking what your mentee wants from the relationship, discussing what you're willing to do, and reaching consensus. You should keep up with their work, so establish a cadence for communication—and clarify the procedure for how and when the person can contact you urgently. And make it clear that accountability isn't optional: Educate mentees about your profession's standards, since any second-rate work will affect your reputation. By setting expectations this way, you'll protect your time—and set up the relationship for success.

Adapted from "6 Things Every Mentor Should Do,"
by Vineet Chopra and Sanjay Saint

Help an Employee Recapture Their Motivation

Helping an employee regain their motivation is easier if you know why they lost it. Talk to the person about what you've been seeing; make clear that your intention is to understand their perspective, not scold them. If you hear that the employee doesn't think their work aligns with their values, help them draw connections. If the person feels they lack the expertise their work requires, point out when they've overcome challenges and brainstorm ways to build new skills. Or if the person isn't sure why they're struggling, encourage them to do some reflection. Identify the problems together and discuss how to move forward productively.

Adapted from "4 Reasons Good Employees Lose Their Motivation,"
by Richard E. Clark and Bror Saxberg

To Lead Well, Delegate

Sometimes you may feel tempted to roll up your sleeves and do everything yourself. But your time and resources are finite, so how you delegate will determine how effective you are as a leader. To get better at delegating, practice four things:

1. Assessing which tasks truly need to be done by you

2. Clarifying the scope of the contribution you're asking for

3. Explaining to your team why a task matters in the bigger picture

4. Involving yourself as much or as little as someone needs

With these principles in mind, the work will get done and you will be free to focus your energy where you're needed most.

———

Adapted from "To Be a Great Leader, You Have to Learn
How to Delegate Well," by Jesse Sostrin

Make It Safer for People to Give You Honest Feedback

As a leader, you need honest feedback to grow, but often what you get is vague or isn't tied to specific behaviors. So build a culture where your employees can be frank, especially about sensitive topics. Tell them you want both positive and negative comments—and resist the urge to respond when they share them. Simply listen and reflect. To get people talking, use open-ended questions such as "What did you hear when I shared my strategy?" or "How did it feel when I sent that email?" Thank your team for their candid responses and use their feedback to make necessary changes.

Adapted from "How Leaders Can Get Honest, Productive Feedback," by Jennifer Porter

To Manage Your Boss, Know Them

To work effectively with your boss, understand the context of their job. Key things to learn are your manager's goals, pressures, strengths, and weaknesses. For example, what are your boss's objectives, both organizationally and personally? What pressures are they under from peers and their own boss? What's your boss's preferred working style? What do they do well—and not so well? How do they like to get information—email, meetings, instant messages? It's important to gain this understanding when you have a new boss, but it's also helpful to consider on an ongoing basis, since your boss's priorities and concerns change over time.

Adapted from "Managing Your Boss,"
by John J. Gabarro and John P. Kotter

Articulate Your Personal Philosophy

Worrying about what other people think of you can be paralyzing. You stop taking chances—and your career suffers. To fight these anxieties, develop a personal philosophy—a phrase or sentence that articulates who you are. Ask yourself: What values drive your actions? What helps you perform best? How do you want to live your life? Look for common threads and use the results to define your personal philosophy. Someone who's focused on reaching their full potential, for example, could remind themselves: "Always compete" or "Never stop getting better." When something at work lowers your confidence, let your philosophy remind you why you do what you do.

Adapted from "How to Stop Worrying About What Other People Think of You," by Michael Gervais

Yes, Women Get Biased Feedback

"A safe space for learning, experimentation, and community is critical in leadership development programs for women. Consider performance feedback, which is necessary for growth and advancement but full of trip wires for women. Research has amply demonstrated that accomplished, high-potential women who are evaluated as competent managers often fail the likability test, whereas competence and likability tend to go hand in hand for similarly accomplished men. Supervisors routinely give high-performing women some version of the message 'You need to trim your sharp elbows.' Creating a safe setting—a coaching relationship, a . . . leadership program, a support group of peers—in which women can interpret these messages is critical to their leadership identity development."

Adapted from "Women Rising: The Unseen Barriers,"
by Herminia Ibarra, Robin J. Ely, and Deborah M. Kolb

Overcome Executive Isolation

Leave the Bubble

The loneliness you might feel as a senior leader may seem like a small price to pay for the rewards, recognition, and power. But being isolated can compromise your decision-making and effectiveness. One way to overcome this condition is to get out of your bubble. You're surrounded by the trappings of your position—client dinners, long-term-strategy sessions, frequent travel—and you need to periodically escape. Taking breaks to listen to stakeholders will keep you connected to what, and who, matters. So seek opportunities to interact with customers to learn their concerns. Talk to employees at all levels about their challenges. Hold town halls to let people ask you tough questions.

Adapted from "How to Overcome Executive Isolation," by Ron Ashkenas

Strategies for Introverts

Act Like an Extrovert—Sparingly

Extrovert employees are paid more, promoted faster, and rated more positively, according to research from the University of Scarborough and the University of Minnesota. How, then, do you succeed as an introvert leader? One way is to act like an extrovert—selectively. Think ahead about situations where you'll need to be "on," such as a pitch meeting with a prospective client or a schmooze-heavy cocktail reception, and block out time to rest before and after. You know your social energy is finite, so be strategic and proactive about when and how to deploy it. Waiting to act until you have an "extroversion hangover" isn't sustainable.

Adapted from "Stop Telling Introverts to Act Like Extroverts,"
by Evy Kuijpers, Joeri Hofmans, and Bart Wille

Get Your Project Team on the Same Page

Misalignment on project teams occurs naturally and continuously. Alignment, on the other hand, requires deliberate guidance, collaboration, and communication—and the success of the project depends on it. That's why you need regular, frank conversations with your team about what you're all working toward. Five questions, asked openly and earnestly, will help keep everyone on the same page:

1. What is your understanding of the project?

2. What concerns do you have?

3. How do you see your role?

4. What do you need?

5. How would you describe your current commitment to the project?

The answers will tell you how aligned your team is—or isn't. If needed, have a group discussion to get everyone on board.

Adapted from "5 Questions to Get Your Project Team on the Same Page," by Timothy R. Clark

The Persuasive Power of Peers

People are more likely to follow someone who's similar to them. That's why, when you need to be persuasive, an effective approach is to use "peer power"—enlisting an employee whom others respect and trust to support your cause. Great salespeople understand this dynamic, which is why they use testimonials from customers who are similar to the prospective client they're trying to woo. So if you're selling colleagues on a new corporate initiative, for example, don't just rely on its own merits. Ask a respected peer who's on board with the change to speak up for it. You'll be more convincing if you exert horizontal, not just vertical, influence.

Adapted from "Harnessing the Science of Persuasion,"
by Robert B. Cialdini

Good Managers Lead Teams, Not Individuals

New managers often fail, at least initially, because they have misconceptions about what it means to be a boss. One of these myths is that managing a team well is only about supporting employees one-on-one and keeping each person happy and productive. But that approach can lead to overly focusing on individual performance and not paying enough attention to developing team culture and group performance. For your team to succeed, keep in mind how decisions and policies will affect the group, not just each person, and set norms and values that will help everyone thrive. After all, you're not just leading individuals—you're leading a team.

Adapted from "Becoming the Boss,"
by Linda A. Hill

When Growth Plateaus

Share Your Goals

When you become a leader, it's easy for your growth to plateau. Your goals are more nebulous (manage a team, run a function), and endless requests for your time can steal attention from your top priorities. To continue growing, try publicly sharing your goals. Telling people what you're aiming to do both keeps your goals top of mind and creates social pressure for you to follow through. You can also form a work group with friends or colleagues to encourage and push one another. Having the support of a small community builds your resilience and likelihood of success.

Adapted from "3 Strategies for Holding Yourself
Accountable," by Diana Kander

Prepare for a Negative Spotlight Before It's on You

Becoming the target of widespread public criticism can be your worst nightmare when you're a leader. It's not something they teach in school. So prepare in advance for a moment when fingers are pointed your way. Think about the values you'll want to guide you, and how you'll want to handle your emotions during a difficult, complicated time. Also, consider the kinds of messages you'll want to convey—both inside your company and outside it, and verbally as well as nonverbally. Ask yourself how you'll want to look back on the situation once it's over, and what you'll wish you'd done.

What kind of a leader do you want to be when public criticism comes your way?

Adapted from "How Leaders Should Handle Public
Criticism," by Ron Carucci

How Humble Are You?

Humility is one of the best antidotes to power's corrupting effects. Although you can't accurately assess how humble you are, seven questions can help you think about the role of humility in your life:

1. Do I seek feedback, even if it's critical?

2. Do I admit when I don't know how to do something?

3. Do I acknowledge when others have more knowledge or skills than I do?

4. Do I take note of others' strengths?

5. Do I compliment others on their strengths?

6. Do I show appreciation for others' contributions?

7. Am I willing to learn from others?

Use the answers to identify areas you need to develop.

Adapted from "Don't Let Power Corrupt You,"
by Julie Battilana and Tiziana Casciaro

The Ethical Risk of Not Sleeping

"Leaders' devaluation of sleep may also cause followers to behave less ethically. Bosses who systematically eschewed rest—in comparison to other managers—rated their [people] as less likely to do the right thing [in our research]. We suspect this wasn't just a matter of the sleep-deprived leaders' giving tougher ratings; it's likely that employees were actually behaving in less moral ways as a result of the workplace environment or their own sleep deprivation. Indeed, in previous studies we've shown that lack of sleep is directly linked to lapses in ethics."

Adapted from "Sleep Well, Lead Better,"
by Christopher M. Barnes

What's Your Leadership Style?

Democratic

Your personal leadership style has a powerful impact on your organization. One type of leadership that has positive effects on an organization's working environment and results is the democratic style. Democratic leaders get people's buy-in and ideas, which builds trust, respect, and commitment. And they listen to employees' concerns, which helps keep morale high. The democratic style is ideal when you're uncertain about the best direction to take and need input from your team. It can fail, though, when it results in endless meetings where consensus remains elusive, leaving employees feeling confused and leaderless. Think about what style a situation calls for, and whether your current approach is working well or may need an adjustment.

Adapted from "Leadership That Gets Results,"
by Daniel Goleman

When Work Is Overwhelming

Question Expectations

When you have too much to do, you may feel anxious any time you're not working. But a huge to-do list doesn't have to overwhelm you. One strategy for managing stress is to check your assumptions about others' expectations. We often make up rules about how fast we need to reply to emails or requests for our time. Instead, ask people when they need a reply, or tell them when you'll get back to them. And practice setting boundaries about responding to messages outside of business hours. The reality of when someone wants a reply may be more generous than whatever you're imagining.

Adapted from "5 Things to Do When You Feel Overwhelmed
by Your Workload," by Alice Boyes

The Most Effective Leaders Learn Everywhere

Your development as a leader shouldn't only happen at work. The most effective leaders learn all the time and everywhere, suggests research published in the *Academy of Management Review*. Being a parent, an athlete on a recreational sports team, a volunteer—all these roles involve an element of leadership, including the possibility of trying out new leadership behaviors to see what works for you.

In what areas of your life—other than work—could you learn more about and develop your leadership skills?

Adapted from "How Busy People Can Develop Leadership
Skills," by Darja Kragt

Your Leadership Voice

Built on Clarity

Cultivating your leadership voice requires building the capacity to respond authentically, constructively, and effectively, no matter the situation or audience. One aspect of your voice is clarity. Amid an endless number of possible priorities, part of your job is to decide what you and your team need to focus on *right now*—and what can wait. You might, for example, pursue projects urgently if they're highly connected to the business's strategy, or if you want them to be among your top achievements for the year. Leaders who fail to provide this clarity risk falling short on their most important wins and spreading their teams thin.

How do you communicate what your top priorities are?

Adapted from "You Don't Just Need One Leadership Voice—
You Need Many," by Amy Jen Su

Build Skills That AI Can't Copy

Avoid Predictability

AI tools may compete with the lower and middle ends of many professions, such as copywriting and design. So it's critical to develop yourself in ways that AI can't copy. One way is to embrace serendipity and your personality. AI is a prediction engine: It's not generating insights; it's guessing what may come next. You, however, have the capacity to be creative and to draw unexpected connections. Maybe you'll use AI tools to gather ideas and knowledge, but your unique interests and experiences are what will synthesize them into something new. When everyone else is overly relying on AI, the best way to stand out is to sound like no one except yourself.

Adapted from "5 Ways to Future-Proof Your Career in the Age of AI,"
by Dorie Clark and Tomas Chamorro-Premuzic

What Successful People Do

Focus on Getting Better

Why have you been so successful in reaching some of your goals but not others? Even brilliant, highly accomplished people aren't great at understanding why they succeed or fail. But successful people do a few things differently, according to decades of research on achievement. One is focusing on getting better, rather than being good. If you believe traits like intelligence are fixed, then you'll set goals that are about proving yourself, rather than learning something new. Measuring yourself on incremental improvement will help you take obstacles or setbacks in stride and reach your full potential.

Adapted from "Nine Things Successful People
Do Differently," by Heidi Grant

Expand Your Definition of Best Job Candidate

When you're hiring, you know which skills and experiences you want candidates to have. But if everyone on your team shares similar backgrounds, they're more likely to think like each other too. That means they view problems and solutions in similar ways, which could make your team's output less creative. Diversity, on the other hand, is linked to greater innovation and performance; McKinsey found that more-diverse companies have higher profits than their more-homogeneous counterparts. So building teams where people have different skill sets and life experiences can literally pay off—for you and for less obvious, but perfectly capable, candidates.

How can you expand your view of candidates?

Adapted from "Why You Should Invest in Unconventional Talent," by Debbie Ferguson and Fredrick "Flee" Lee

Prioritize Psychological Safety for Black Women

Psychological safety at work can be harder for Black women to feel. To better support the Black women in your company, you can take a few steps. Train managers in cultural humility, equitable decision-making, and understanding racial trauma. Do a salary audit to ensure Black women are paid equitably. You could also invite Black employees to share their experiences, including the challenges they encounter both at work and outside work, if they feel comfortable doing so. Examine policies around coaching, 360-degree feedback, and performance management to uncover biases that hold people back. And revisit your company's DEI commitments, to ensure they address different factors of employees' identities, particularly race.

Adapted from "Creating Psychological Safety for Black Women at Your Company," by Agatha Agbanobi and T. Viva Asmelash

The Solution to the Skills Gap Isn't More Training

"We know that, after decades of trying, skills related to lean manufacturing, agile development, and overcoming unconscious bias, just to name a few, are woefully under-adopted in most organizations. . . . More training is not the answer. We can't simply send employees to workshops focused on whatever proficiency is fashionable at the moment and expect to get results. What is essential is to build coherent skills-based strategies. We must think seriously about which specific skills are to be targeted, who has to learn them, and what mix of education, experience, and exposure will be effective to create the skills-based organizations we need to meet the challenges of the future."

Adapted from "Help Your Employees Develop the Skills They Really Need," by Greg Satell, Abhijit Bhaduri, and Todd McLees

Focus on What's Important, Not on What's Urgent

Manage Your Anxiety

Your to-do list has both important and urgent tasks. It's easy to work on what's due soonest, but sometimes the important projects need your attention more. To prioritize what matters most, manage your feelings of anxiety. Doing important tasks often involves considering what could go wrong, which isn't fun to think about and so could make you avoid them. Get comfortable with tolerating uncomfortable feelings by recognizing and labeling them when they arise. Being able to say "I'm feeling nervous about not doing this well" will help you keep that feeling in check and make it easier to go outside your comfort zone.

Adapted from "How to Focus on What's Important,
Not Just What's Urgent," by Alice Boyes

It's Not Always the Size of the Goal That Motivates People

Work doesn't have to involve alleviating poverty or curing cancer to feel meaningful. Jobs with less societal importance can matter if they contribute value to something or someone that's important to employees. Meaning could be as simple as making a high-quality product, providing a service to a community, or reducing inefficiencies in a production process. Whether the goals are lofty or modest, they can supercharge someone's work life—if they matter to the employee and it's clear how the person's efforts contribute to them.

What gives your role meaning? How are you helping your people feel meaning in their jobs?

Adapted from "The Power of Small Wins,"
by Teresa M. Amabile and Steven J. Kramer

Don't Be a Victim of Your Success

Take a Wider View

To keep performing at your best, you must overcome the barriers that accompany your success. One barrier is having narrow frames of reference because you have one primary area of expertise. Every industry has its own specific knowledge, jargon, and methods of thinking. Your expertise may have served you well in your career so far, but don't assume it's the only expertise you'll need. If you look at all problems the same way, you'll try to solve them all the same way, which eventually will limit your effectiveness.

How can you broaden your perspective to view problems and solutions in new ways?

Adapted from "Want to Change the World? Don't Let Your Own Success Get in the Way," by Rosabeth Moss Kanter

Break Your Career-Limiting Habit

Schedule Yourself

We all have a career-limiting habit, such as procrastinating or using our phones when we should be connecting with others. But people who overcome bad habits take control of the circumstances that feed them, according to research from Crucial Learning. One way to do this is to schedule yourself. Humans have a default bias: If a box is checked on a website, we're likely to leave it checked. So program defaults into your life. Don't just decide you want to practice your presentations before your quarterly review. Put practice time on your calendar and stick to it. You're more likely to spend an hour rehearsing if it's your default plan.

Adapted from "Trick Yourself into Breaking a Bad Habit,"
by Joseph Grenny

Want a High-Performing Team?

Build Social Connections

To build a high-performing team, don't overlook the importance of social connections. Greater connectedness and performance go hand in hand, according to research from learning and development company ignite80. To encourage genuine relationships, invest time in bonding over nonwork topics. Discussing hobbies, families, and TV shows can reveal shared interests, which yield closer friendships and better teamwork. You should also make appreciation a team norm. Recognition can be more motivating than monetary rewards, and it shouldn't come just from you—encourage peers to applaud each other's efforts. Sometimes praise is even more valued when it doesn't come from the boss.

———————

Adapted from "5 Things High-Performing Teams
Do Differently," by Ron Friedman

Get Off the Hedonistic Treadmill

Your brain is wired to reward you with a sense of pleasure when you achieve your goals. But brains are also wired to seek balance from extreme emotional states—meaning the high wears off and you're left with an empty longing to repeat the experience, like walking on a treadmill of dopamine. That's why so many people try to find happiness in pursuing money, status, or fame. They know the rush of success won't last, but it feels good while it does.

Rather than chasing the momentary boost of triumph again and again, how can you pursue more meaningful satisfaction in your life?

———————————

Adapted from "Why Success Doesn't Lead to Satisfaction,"
by Ron Carucci

To Be a Great Leader, Be a Great Coach

Coaching is about finding ways to spark growth-oriented insights in an employee. To do it effectively, you need to ask questions instead of providing answers, support people instead of judging them, and facilitate their development instead of dictating what they do. Try the GROW model:

1. Ask what *goal* the person wants to achieve.

2. Ask about the goal's *realities*—its who, what, when, and where.

3. Help the employee think broadly and deeply to explore different *options*.

4. Check the person's *will* to act by confirming they're committed to following through on the chosen option.

Repeat these steps until you jointly reach a solution they feel confident about.

Adapted from "The Leader as Coach," by Herminia Ibarra
and Anne Scoular

Transition to Senior Leadership

Become an Architect

When you shift from leading a function to leading an enterprise, you must navigate a tricky set of changes in your leadership focus and skills. One change is becoming an architect. As you move up the org chart, you must think not in terms of individual jobs or functions but in terms of *systems*—how key elements of the company fit together. That means knowing the principles of organizational change and change management, as well as the many interdependencies among functions. Don't believe you can change one element without affecting many others. To prepare yourself, seek out trainings in organizational change, so you'll be able to make thoughtful decisions when the time comes.

Adapted from "How Managers Become Leaders,"
by Michael D. Watkins

Unethical Behavior Can Be Contagious

Big ethical lapses grow out of small bad behaviors. That's why you should watch for two types of unethical actions on your team. One type is how company culture affects your employees. We tend to mimic the values of those around us, so if some employees habitually exaggerate last month's numbers, others may do it too. Revisit your norms and consider how they're influencing your team. The second type is using high-stakes deadlines to justify bad behavior. Bending the rules when the pressure is on can be tempting, so talk to your team about your ethical standards. Discuss what's OK, what isn't, and where the line is.

Adapted from "The Psychology Behind Unethical Behavior,"
by Merete Wedell-Wedellsborg

Questions to Ask Yourself

Am I Getting the Feedback I Need?

Through the ups and downs of your career, regularly asking yourself a few questions can help you stay on track with your goals and priorities. One of those questions is: Do you have people who will tell you things you need to hear? Your team is in a better position than your boss to tell you how you're doing, but employees may be scared to offer their honest feedback. Make a concerted, persistent effort to ask what you can do better, and then to act on it to show you really listened.

How are you building a culture where people feel safe to give each other constructive feedback, regardless of their job titles?

Adapted from "What to Ask the Person in the Mirror,"
by Robert Steven Kaplan

To Move On from Change

Work Through Hard Emotions

Sometimes a big change—personal or professional—upends your identity. Working through your negative feelings about the shift can help you move forward. It's easy to get stuck in emotions associated with your old life. For example, maybe you're angry and ashamed that you were laid off from a beloved job. Acknowledging those feelings, and cultivating opposing positive ones, can help. If being laid off led you to create your own business, or spend more time with your children or friends, that could be a major source of pride. The goal isn't to push away negative emotions—it's to make peace with them and refocus on more helpful ones.

Adapted from "When a Major Life Change Upends Your Sense of Self," by Madeline Toubiana, Trish Ruebottom, and Luciana Turchick Hakak

Better Succession Planning

Develop Rising Stars

Succession planning is complex and important to the ongoing success of your company. You know the skills that top executives need: strategic orientation, market insight, and competence at collaborating with and influencing others, to name a few. To make sure your company's leadership pipeline is robust, identify people who have those capabilities—or the potential to develop them, signaled by curiosity, insight, engagement, and determination, along with emotional intelligence, which encompasses flexibility, adaptability, self-control, and relationship management. Once you've identified strong candidates, give them challenging rotations and stretch assignments. When you expose your highest-potential people to new geographies, businesses, situations, and functions, you can become a leadership factory.

Adapted from "The High Cost of Poor Succession Planning,"
by Claudio Fernández-Aráoz, Gregory Nagel, and Carrie Green

Admit Your DEI Blunder

Sometimes your efforts to be inclusive will backfire. Maybe you use language that some find offensive or problematic, or you neglect to name every group that is suffering an injustice. To respond effectively, start by owning your mistake. Don't try to fix it immediately. Instead, listen to others' feedback, take responsibility for what you said—or didn't say—apologize, and commit to doing better. Demonstrate genuine curiosity about the nature of your misstep. Ask questions about your word choices and use this opportunity to better understand another culture or point of view. Your goal is to lead by example: The more you engage with these kinds of issues, the more your team will too.

Adapted from "When Your Efforts to Be Inclusive Misfire,"
by Daisy Auger-Dominguez

Are You Neglecting Your Life Outside of Work?

A leadership role can take over your life if you let it. And by the time you realize that your devotion to work has hurt your partner, children, friends—whoever is most important to you—it may be too late. Neglect your personal relationships, and they will suffer. Fail to prioritize your self-care, and it too will languish, which could lead to any number of physical or mental health problems. There will always be more work to do; don't make choices that endanger the life you want to have in the years and decades to come.

How can you find a better balance between the things that matter most to you?

Adapted from "How to Be a Visionary Leader and Still Have a Personal Life," by David Lancefield

New Leaders, Anticipate Concerns

When you transition into leadership, you need to show employees, bosses, and peers what you bring to the table. One group of questions you'll face are about how you'll lead—changes you'll make, team policies you'll have, and how secure you'll make employees feel about their jobs. People want to know your plans and who will be affected, as well as basics like how you want employees to communicate with and bring problems to you. These kinds of questions help people figure out how to feel about you as a leader. By thinking through what matters to and worries different groups, you can tailor your responses to start these new relationships effectively.

Adapted from "Stepping into a Leadership Role?
Be Ready to Tell Your Story," by David Sluss

To Help Women Get Ahead

Support New Hires

As a leader, you know that women are still dramatically under-represented in positions of power: Few *Fortune* 500 companies are led by women, and even fewer by women of color. One way to reduce the barriers holding women back is to give new hires the support they need. Be careful that women aren't positioned as outliers or tokens, which will undermine them from the start. Consider your company's "real" power structures and whether they exclude women. Proactively help them build the kinds of relationships and networks that are critical to success. And encourage white male leaders to mentor, advocate for, and counter bias about women, especially women of color.

Adapted from "How to Close the Gender Gap,"
by Colleen Ammerman and Boris Groysberg

Respond to Mistakes with Curiosity

One way to build psychological safety on your team is to create an environment where it's OK to make mistakes. People won't take a risk if they're worried about being shut down or blamed when something goes wrong. So when an employee messes up, withhold judgment and instead express curiosity about what happened. A learning mindset is essential here: Recognize that you don't have all the facts, and ask questions about the person's thinking and assumptions. Aim to understand how and why they made the mistake, so you both can learn.

Adapted from "What Is Psychological Safety?,"
by Amy Gallo

How to Make Your Employees Quit

Assign Easy Tasks

Losing an employee hurts morale and productivity, and replacing people who leave is expensive. One mistake that can lead your people to quit is assigning boring or easy tasks. When employees don't have enough to do, they lose motivation and engagement. If someone asks for more, or more-challenging work, discuss how to extend their capabilities and what they could take on. Ask about their interests and passions, and use the answers to assign tasks that will enhance their knowledge and skills. Also consider creating a learning agenda for them with target goals and a road map of how to reach them. This plan will help both of you track their progress.

Adapted from "8 Things Leaders Do That Make
Employees Quit," by Jon Christiansen

Sometimes Leading Well Is Boring

"What is good management? There's no single, comprehensive answer. But in our research, we focus on three facets: target-setting, incentives, and monitoring. Well-managed companies set reasonable, strategic goals; set their staff up to contribute to them; and measure their progress. Call it boring if you like—I call it good business. . . . This view of leadership is harder to put on magazine covers, and it is therefore often forgotten. But ignoring the complex relationship between leaders and their organizations is bad for investors, consumers, and ultimately for managers and CEOs, too."

Adapted from "The Myth of the Brilliant, Charismatic Leader," by Raffaella Sadun

Develop Your Learning Agility

Make Connections

If you rely on the same assumptions and behavioral repertoires you've used for years as a leader, you are prone to stagnate, underperform, or derail, according to research from Korn Ferry. The solution is to develop learning agility, the capacity for rapid, continuous learning. One method is to find connections between seemingly unrelated domains. Think about an area you have knowledge of but that's not tied to your work. Then consider how your knowledge and expertise could be applied to that area in innovative ways. For example, can you use principles from leadership development in your side gig or hobby? This activity forces you to expand your thinking and bring creativity to new challenges.

Adapted from "4 Ways to Become a Better Learner,"
by Monique Valcour

Find Small Ways to Have More Time

Gaining back time in small ways is good for your happiness, stress levels, and health, according to research from Harvard Business School. You might, for example, buy back time by taking a ride-hailing service to work instead of driving, and use that time to catch up on email. When you're feeling caught up, try to leave work early and spend time on fulfilling activities. You can also ask to move back deadlines. That may feel perilous, but proactively managing your schedule is more productive than pushing yourself to meet a deadline that feels out of reach. That's especially true when having a little more time would help you do your very best work.

Adapted from "Time for Happiness,"
by Ashley Whillans

Great Mentors Head Off Rifts

You're almost guaranteed to have a disagreement or misunderstanding with a mentee at some point. It's usually possible to repair any issues—but taking the lead is your responsibility as a mentor. Don't let a problem fester or escalate; as soon as you're aware of it, take action to keep the relationship on track. Talk to the person about what happened and what their perspective was about it; aim to uncover their motives, and resist rushing to judgment. You're trying to prevent more problems in the future, so learn what caused this one. Open, frank relationships are what make mentoring work; if you don't have one, start now.

Adapted from "6 Things Every Mentor Should Do,"
by Vineet Chopra and Sanjay Saint

Learn to Control Your Attention

"Attention is the basis of the most essential of leadership skills— emotional, organizational, and strategic intelligence. And never has it been under greater assault. The constant onslaught of incoming data leads to sloppy shortcuts—triaging our e-mail by reading only the subject lines, skipping many of our voice mails, skimming [documents] and reports. Not only do our habits of attention make us less effective, but the sheer volume of all those messages leaves us too little time to reflect on what they really mean. . . . Learn to master your attention, and you will be in command of where you, and your organization, focus."

Adapted from "The Focused Leader,"
by Daniel Goleman

What Great Questions Do

Broaden Others' Thinking

A great question can help you learn more about a task, unlock hidden opportunities, deliver better results, and mitigate unforeseen risks. One mark of a great question is that it invites others to broaden their thinking. Challenging peers' and colleagues' beliefs can open up the conversation and uncover new solutions. For example, don't say, "You've mentioned you want to improve employee satisfaction to improve performance in turn. What are your next steps?" Say, "Studies show that engagement is a better predictor of performance than satisfaction is. Lots of factors contribute to engagement—how can we tackle a number of those?"

———————————

Adapted from "The Art of Asking Great Questions," by Tijs Besieux

Focus DEI Efforts on Fairness

Diversity initiatives can cause backlash because they feel like a judgment of employees' inherent skills, competence, and goodness. That's why you should frame your DEI efforts around fairness. Making a business case for them could alienate marginalized groups, and increasing diversity for its own sake may do the same for advantaged groups. Instead, stress that DEI efforts are about reducing unfairness at work and will benefit everyone. Highlight the organizational resources that are available to anyone (for example, learning resources and leadership coaching) to underscore that all employees deserve a chance to succeed.

Adapted from "To Avoid DEI Backlash, Focus on Changing Systems—Not People," by Lily Zheng

Storytelling to Drive Change

Provide a Mandate

When your organization needs to make a big change, stories can help you convey not only why it needs to transform but also what the future will look like in specific, vivid terms. Good storytelling does four things. One of them is providing a mandate for change. Your rationale must address the problem you're trying to solve and present the cost of not solving it. It also should give people good reasons to press on with the effort over the long term. It's easy for employees, teams, and organizations to stick to the comfort of familiar behaviors; your answers must be persuasive enough to override that impulse and encourage them to look ahead.

Adapted from "Storytelling That Drives Bold Change,"
by Frances X. Frei and Anne Morriss

Focusing as a Leader

On the World

One of your primary tasks as a leader is to direct attention. To do that, first learn to focus your own attention, in three broad ways: on yourself, on others, and on the wider world. Focusing on the world means being a good listener and a good questioner. It also means being open to how seemingly unrelated information can be brought together, and being able to imagine how choices you make today will play out in the future. Leaders who exemplify these traits—or who learn to—can put ideas together in new ways and open up untapped potential.

Adapted from "The Focused Leader,"
by Daniel Goleman

The Persuasive Power of Consistency

People tend to follow through with on-the-record commitments. That's why, when you need to be persuasive, an effective approach is to get *active*, *public*, and *voluntary* buy-in. Active means someone agrees to something verbally or in writing. Public means they do so in front of others. And voluntary means they aren't coerced into it. To convince employees to embrace a new planning process, for example, ask them to email you ideas for integrating it into their work (active); share their thoughts to start forming a team strategy (public); and discuss how the process will help them meet deadlines (voluntary).

When commitments are framed this way, people are more likely to honor them.

Adapted from "Harnessing the Science of Persuasion," by Robert B. Cialdini

Don't Let Your To-Do List Distract You from Leading Your Team

If you're struggling to balance your individual work and the work of leading your team, reset your priorities. Seek out leaders who find that balance and ask how they do it. You can also get their feedback on your efforts. Use it to think about ways to give employees what they need, whether that's having regular career development conversations or closing your laptop to focus in one-on-one meetings. Over the next few weeks, notice when you feel a task or deadline pulling your attention away from an employee. Remind yourself to focus on the people you're leading— you'll get back to your to-do list soon enough.

Adapted from "Why Highly Efficient Leaders Fail,"
by Rebecca Zucker

Leading Through Uncertainty

Choose Courage over Comfort

When the world feels uncertain and chaotic, you have no clue what will happen next. How can you reassure employees and help them stay focused? One way to lead well in these conditions is to be courageous when you'd rather do what feels safe. Choosing courage—such as making business decisions based on your values, rather than quick profits—can feel vulnerable; you'll likely face criticism and make mistakes. But standing for what you believe in invites others to do the same. Courage can give you the strength to feel the fear and to move forward anyway.

Adapted from "3 Strategies for Leading Through Difficult Times,"
by Rasmus Hougaard, Jacqueline Carter, and Rob Stembridge

Questions to Ask Often

Couldn't We at Least...?

When you ask great questions, you inspire curiosity, creativity, and deeper thinking in yourself and in your employees. One useful question is "Couldn't we at least...?" You've probably had the experience of sitting through a contentious meeting where stakeholders are polarized, progress is stalled, and consensus feels like a pipe dream. Asking "Couldn't we at least...?" can help you and your colleagues get unstuck on an issue. Perhaps you might first find some common ground by asking "Couldn't we at least agree on some basic principles?" or "Couldn't we at least begin, and reevaluate at a later time?"

Adapted from "5 Questions Leaders Should Be Asking
All the Time," by James E. Ryan

Strategies for Introverts

Plan Your Schedule Around Your Energy Levels

Extrovert employees are paid more, promoted faster, and rated more positively, according to research from the University of Scarborough and the University of Minnesota. How, then, do you succeed as an introvert leader? One way is to plan your schedule to support your energy levels. Think about how drained different social situations (meetings, client dinners) make you feel, and how much time you need to recharge. Then, as much as possible, block out alone time accordingly. For example, set aside a few minutes after a big presentation to meditate or journal, or schedule short breaks throughout the day. Whatever methods you use, be proactive—waiting until you're depleted will only make things worse.

———————

Adapted from "Stop Telling Introverts to Act Like Extroverts,"
by Evy Kuijpers, Joeri Hofmans, and Bart Wille

Nurture Progress

To ensure that your team is motivated and committed, and to help them make daily progress in their jobs, research from Teresa Amabile and Steven Kramer suggests using *nourishers*, events such as demonstrations of respect and words of encouragement. These include acts of interpersonal support, such as recognition, encouragement, emotional comfort, and opportunities for affiliation. Their research found that nourishers occur frequently on days when employees report feeling at their best, based on their mood, emotions, and motivation, and that they can lend greater meaning to work. All this may sound like Management 101—but research also shows how often even attentive managers forget about or ignore the importance of basic respect and consideration.

Adapted from "The Power of Small Wins,"
by Teresa M. Amabile and Steven J. Kramer

Patience Is a Virtue— and an Essential Leadership Skill

It's hard to be a good leader if you aren't patient, for a few reasons. When you're facing setbacks or difficulties, you can't keep others calm if you can't stay calm yourself. In addition, new strategies and solutions to problems take time to implement; quick fixes won't always get the job done. And, of course, our always-on working world values immediate replies and constant connectivity. Often, though, success comes from being methodical, careful, and (yes) slow—whether you're evaluating a new idea or making a big decision.

How patient do you think you are? Would your employees agree? How can you develop this vital skill further?

Adapted from "Becoming a More Patient Leader,"
by David Sluss

Develop a Strategy for Your Career

Grade Yourself

To ensure a meaningful career, create a long-term strategy for it. One step is to grade your current work situation. Don't just rely on your gut to evaluate your job satisfaction. Ask four questions: Are you learning? Are you having an impact? Are you having fun? Are you being rewarded? Spend time thinking through your responses and what they tell you. If you aren't satisfied with the answers, consider how to improve them—and whether that can be done in your current job or whether you should look elsewhere.

Adapted from "Developing a Strategy for a Life of Meaningful Labor," by Brian Fetherstonhaugh

Leading as Your Team Grows

Choose Your Battles

As your team grows, your processes and approach must evolve in several ways. One is by choosing your battles. The more projects you oversee, the more likely it is that something is going wrong. Maybe an initiative is behind schedule, a miscommunication needs clearing up, or employees are competing over resources. But your time and attention are limited, perfection isn't an option, and you can't do everything—so learn to (perhaps ruthlessly) prioritize. What's most important to tackle today, and what isn't? The number of demands you face every day can feel overwhelming; get comfortable with letting less-essential things wait.

Adapted from "As Your Team Gets Bigger, Your Leadership Style Has to Adapt," by Julie Zhuo

Keep Your Writing Simple

When you're writing for work, you may think you need to sound impressive by using jargon or fancy words. But overblown language doesn't make you sound smart, and it may turn off readers. Instead, aim for a conversational but professional tone. Use short, familiar words and explain your ideas in a straightforward and simple manner. Formatting can help too: Highlight key takeaways with headings, bullet points, and italics or bolding. And keep your sentences and paragraphs short—if they're crammed full of ideas, the reader may just give up. Your message will likely be read on a phone, possibly while someone is busy or distracted, so it should be understandable at a glance.

———————————

Adapted from "Writing About Business (Without Being a Bore),"
by Mike Reed

To Build Courage, Start Small

"I realized that one isn't born with courage. One develops it by doing small courageous things—in the way that if one sets out to pick up a 100-pound bag of rice, one would be advised to start with a five-pound bag, then 10 pounds, then 20 pounds, and so forth, until one builds up enough muscle to lift the 100-pound bag. It's the same way with courage. You do small courageous things that require some mental and spiritual exertion."

Adapted from "Life's Work: An Interview with
Maya Angelou," by Alison Beard

Questions to Ask Often

What Truly Matters?

When you ask great questions, you inspire curiosity, creativity, and deeper thinking in yourself and in your employees. One useful question is "What truly matters?" It's not a question you should save for vacation or retirement; it should be a regular conversational prompt, externally and internally. Pose this question to simplify complicated situations, like sensitive personnel issues, and to stay grounded when you have grand ambitions, like an organizational restructuring. Asking it often will not only make your work life smoother but also help you find balance in the broader context of your life.

Adapted from "5 Questions Leaders Should Be Asking
All the Time," by James E. Ryan

Boost Your Versatility

To develop yourself as a leader, you must put in effort to become a more well-rounded person. That requires identifying opposing skills and leadership behaviors (such as being decisive but also empowering others; being demanding but also supportive) and pushing yourself to grow in both—rather than relying on whichever one you're strongest in. The goal is to step beyond what's familiar and comfortable, and what's gotten you to your current position. Less-versatile leaders often have a rigid and narrow view of who they are and think perspectives that clash with their own should be avoided, rather than experimented with and learned from. Great leaders know better.

How can you become more versatile?

———————————

Adapted from "The Best Leaders Are Versatile Ones,"
by Robert B. (Rob) Kaiser

The Benefits of Being an Inclusive Leader

You should think of inclusive traits like humility, curiosity, and empathy as critical leadership capabilities, rather than simply desirable ones. Why? How leaders act can make a huge difference in whether employees feel included and psychologically safe; inclusive leaders also see double-digit increases in measures of team performance, decision-making quality, and team collaboration, according to Deloitte. And inclusive leaders cut employee attrition risk by 76%, according to Boston Consulting Group.

How can you keep developing inclusive traits in yourself?

Adapted from "What Makes an Inclusive Leader?,"
by Wei Zheng, Jennifer Kim, Ronit Kark, and Lisa Mascolo

Fight Career Malaise with an Ongoing Perspective

Work can feel like an endless conveyor belt of projects, especially if you're mid-career. To deal productively with this malaise, shift your perspective. Jobs are full of finite efforts: You prepare the client pitch and then present it; you plan the conference and then host it. So rather than focusing on *fixed* activities (projects), think about *ongoing* ones (what your projects contribute to). For example, when you're working on a deal, you're furthering your company's growth strategy; when you're hosting a conference, you're engaging industry stakeholders. Adjusting your mindset to embrace the ongoing, infinite aspects of work can help defeat a sense of emptiness without changing what you do or how you do it.

Adapted from "Facing Your Mid-Career Crisis," by Kieran Setiya

When Employees Like You, You Seem More Effective

There's an old saying that leadership isn't about being liked, it's about results. But that's not really true anymore. Employees value having leaders who show they care about their people. So work to develop a personal rapport with those you lead—so they'll *want* to follow you. After all, if employees feel connected to you, they're more likely to think you're a good leader, according to research analysis from scholars at Northeastern University, Wake Forest University, and Florida State University. That doesn't mean building relationships should take priority over everything else you need to do. But ignore what people think of you at your peril.

Adapted from "Why Likable Leaders Seem More Effective,"
by Charn McAllister, Sherry Moss, and Mark J. Martinko

Learning: The Antidote to Obsolescence

In the past, leaders built their careers by developing deep expertise in a topic or field as they advanced. Today, specialized expertise is less important than being able to learn from others. Think of digital knowledge: Technology evolves so quickly that staying up to date is a challenge. You may or may not need to be a digital expert yourself—but you do need to learn from people who are.

Whose expertise do you need to learn from? What new perspectives could it unlock?

Adapted from "Every Leader Needs to Navigate These 7 Tensions," by Jennifer Jordan, Michael Wade, and Elizabeth Teracino

Your Leadership Voice

Built on Curiosity

Cultivating your leadership voice requires building the capacity to respond authentically, constructively, and effectively, no matter the situation or audience. One aspect of your voice is curiosity. Your role as a leader involves giving direction and making decisions, but be careful not to approach every situation as if you have all the answers. Often, showing curiosity about a problem, and inviting others to share their ideas, is a more constructive approach. You hired smart people; if their perspective differs from yours, find out where they're coming from so that you can reach the best solutions.

How do you express curiosity when you're tackling tough challenges?

Adapted from "You Don't Just Need One Leadership Voice—
You Need Many," by Amy Jen Su

Build Skills That AI Can't Copy

Cultivate Expertise

AI tools may compete with the lower and middle ends of many professions, such as copywriting and design. So it's critical to develop yourself in ways that AI can't copy. One way is to continue cultivating and sharing your knowledge of your field. AI tools are useful for summoning facts almost instantly, but sometimes the "facts" it reports just aren't true. Since AI's accuracy can't always be trusted, developing your reputation as a trustworthy expert has never been more important. Even when AI performs "first draft" functions, trusted humans still need to verify its results. If people know that you know your stuff, you'll be sought out to vet AI's work.

Adapted from "5 Ways to Future-Proof Your Career in the Age of AI,"
by Dorie Clark and Tomas Chamorro-Premuzic

Too Busy at Work?

Make Time to Exercise Anyway

You know that exercise has physical benefits, but there are also professional benefits to being active, found researchers from HKU Business School, Lingnan University, Hong Kong Baptist University, and Fuzhou University. For one, exercise can strengthen your task focus, which supports information processing, attention, and concentration. Task focus is also a strong predictor of self-rated creative performance. These benefits carry over to the *day after* you exercise, which means working out today will make you feel more focused and creative tomorrow. So find ways to integrate physical activity into your routine: It's an investment in your health *and* your career.

Adapted from "To Improve Your Work Performance, Get Some Exercise," by Bonnie Hayden Cheng and Yolanda Na Li

When Your Team's Vibe Is Off

Reset Its Strategies and Roles

If your team is feeling stuck or stale, it could be because employees have lost sight of their purpose and the goals they're working toward. Whether the malaise is due to external factors or internal ones (or both), sometimes your team's strategies and roles need a refresh. Discussing a few questions as a group can help:

1. Is our team strategy aligned with our mandate?

2. What tactics and approaches do we need to revise?

3. What assumptions or new circumstances could endanger our plans?

4. Does anyone need a change in role?

5. How can we adjust people's responsibilities?

The answers can help change what your team does and who carries out specific roles.

Adapted from "20 Questions to Ask When Your Team's
Vibe Is Off," by Liane Davey

Transition to Senior Leadership

Be a Role Model

When you shift from leading a function to leading an enterprise, you must navigate a tricky set of changes in your leadership focus and skills. One change is taking the lead role in the company. People will place a great deal of stock in what you say and do; everyone will look to you for vision, inspiration, and cues about the "right" behaviors and attitudes. To make sure you're sending the messages you want to send, cultivate self-awareness and develop empathy for employees' viewpoints. You're a role model now, so be extra thoughtful about your impact.

Adapted from "How Managers Become Leaders,"
by Michael D. Watkins

Are You Challenging Your Team Enough?

Most people aren't engaged at work. When employees are in the same job for a long time, they can stop growing and lose their motivation. Our brains want to be learning, and to do that they need new challenges to solve. You can build an A-team by optimizing the mix of employees' learning curves: 15% of your people should be just starting to learn new skills, 70% should be honing and practicing their skills, and 15% should be at the high end of mastering them. When someone reaches the top of a learning curve, help them jump to the bottom of another one. Continually learning new things is the secret to engagement.

Adapted from "How to Lose Your Best Employees,"
by Whitney Johnson

Don't Let Perfectionism Derail You

Get Perspective

Perfectionism can push you to deliver excellent work, but it can also increase your anxiety and lower your productivity. To corral your perfectionism, learn when it's time to let go and move on. One tactic is to ask a trusted colleague to help you get perspective. Once you have a draft of whatever you're working on, show it to someone and ask what it needs to be *good enough*—rather than perfect. Follow the feedback you get, and trust what the person says; maybe a task you thought needed 10 hours only needs five. High standards are great, but they shouldn't keep you from getting your work done.

Adapted from "How to Manage Your Perfectionism,"
by Rebecca Knight

Be a Sleep Role Model

"Even if you fail to get enough sleep yourself, you should be careful to promote good sleeping behavior. Your employees are watching you for cues about what is important. Avoid bragging about your own lack of sleep, lest you signal to your subordinates that they, too, should deprioritize sleep. If you absolutely must compose an e-mail at 3 a.m., use a delayed-delivery option so that the message isn't sent until 8 a.m. If you must pull an all-nighter on a project, don't hold that up as exemplary behavior. . . . If instead you make sleep a priority, you will be a more successful leader who inspires better work in your employees."

Adapted from "Sleep Well, Lead Better,"
by Christopher M. Barnes

You Can't Set Strategy Alone

When you're creating a strategy, don't forget that you and other senior leaders aren't the ones who actually implement it—your managers and frontline employees are. So you can't just announce new plans and assume everyone knows what they are and is on board with them. Instead, you have to proactively get input and feedback from people across the org chart, listening to their ideas and concerns and responding meaningfully. Building consensus takes much more than senior leaders saying, "Here's what you should do."

Are there any teams or groups you could get more input from when setting strategy?

Adapted from "Is Your Company as Strategically Aligned as You Think It Is?," by Vikas Mittal, Alessandro Piazza, and Ashwin Malshe

Three Tough Leadership Transitions

As a leader, you may struggle with three kinds of transitions, according to research from executive search consultancy Spencer Stuart:

- **Becoming a leader.** You may be unprepared for the frantic pace or lack a big-picture strategic perspective, for example.

- **Leading organizational transitions.** If you can't also reinvent yourself or your team fast enough, leading high-stakes transformations can be a real risk.

- **Reaching the top.** Once you attain a job you've been working toward for years, you may not know what you're supposed to do next.

Have you struggled with any of these transitions? How did you handle it?

———————

Adapted from "3 Transitions Even the Best Leaders Struggle With," by Cassandra Frangos

Learning to Learn

Ask Questions Like a Toddler

Acquiring new knowledge quickly and continually is a skill that will never be obsolete. One way to do it is to be relentlessly curious. Increase your willingness to tackle new things by asking questions that highlight what you don't know. If you aren't sure how a process works or why teams follow certain guidelines, for example, phrases like "How . . . ?" or "Why . . . ?" or "I wonder if . . ." can prompt you to dig deeper. When children want to understand something, they ask an endless series of "But why?" questions. Do the same with topics you want to know more about.

Adapted from "Learning to Learn,"
by Erika Andersen

When Your Predecessor Was a Star, Be Yourself

Taking over for a respected, successful leader is nerve-racking. But don't try to copy your predecessor's personality or style. Being unapologetically yourself will earn you respect and preempt comparisons. Aim to come across as confident and genuine; you might consider explaining to peers and employees how you plan to lead, including how you'll differ from the previous leader. As time passes, check in on how you're doing by seeking regular feedback from trusted colleagues. Ask what you're doing well and less well, so you can make improvements. And if you need an outside perspective, a mentor or executive coach can provide an objective view of your areas for growth.

Adapted from "How to Succeed When You Have
Big Shoes to Fill," by Rebecca Zucker

Build Your Collaboration Skills

Personal Accountability

Teams are interconnected systems of preferences, skills, experiences, and perspectives. To lead such a complex entity well, you must develop your personal accountability. Doing so involves reflecting on how you respond to challenging situations, including unhealthy patterns such as blaming others, getting defensive, or avoiding an issue. It also includes identifying how your reactions contribute to problems. To build your accountability, recognize when a problem with colleagues or employees arises, and be honest about what your role in it may be. Then take responsibility for addressing the situation. Talk to the person about what's going on, what their perspective is, and how to move forward productively. By being proactive and open, you'll show employees you're dedicated to accountability.

Adapted from "To Improve Your Team, First Work
on Yourself," by Jennifer Porter

What Do You Want Your Days to Look Like?

Early in our careers, we're often focused on doing what it takes to advance. As your skill set and experience open up more options, though, it's worth evaluating how well your job supports the day-to-day life you want. Think about how you'd like to spend your time, who you want to interact with, and what you like doing outside of work. Then consider whether the path you're on aligns with those priorities. If there's a gap, look for ways to shift your responsibilities or schedule accordingly; with bigger disconnects, it may be necessary to change jobs or careers. But don't put off asking these questions—your working years, like your life itself, are finite.

Adapted from "6 Questions to Ask at the Midpoint of Your Career," by Rebecca Knight

The Power of Leading as a Human Being

"The power of leadership lies in our abilities to form personal and meaningful bonds with the people whom we lead. . . . As human beings, we are all driven by basic needs for meaning, happiness, human connectedness, and a desire to contribute positively to others. And leaders that truly understand these needs, and lead in a way that enables these intrinsic motivations, have the keys to enable strong loyalty, engagement, and performance. As leaders, we must be humans before managers."

Adapted from "Why Do So Many Managers Forget They're
Human Beings?," by Rasmus Hougaard, Jacqueline Carter,
and Vince Brewerton

Shape Your Company's Vision

To be a good leader, you must create a unifying vision for the organization. But sometimes building one is more associated with senior executives than with other leaders. No matter your role, you can get hands-on experience in shaping vision. For example, contributing to senior leaders' work, translating the company's mission for your team, and developing a new frontline team strategy may be things you can do in your current role. Any of those tasks can add to your professional development, leading to bigger responsibilities over time.

What vision-shaping opportunities can you seize right now?

Adapted from "You Don't Have to Be CEO to Be a Visionary Leader,"
by Ron Ashkenas and Brook Manville

To Help Women Get Ahead

Improve Compensation and Promotion

As a leader, you know that women are still dramatically under-represented in positions of power: Few *Fortune* 500 companies are led by women, and even fewer by women of color. One way to reduce the barriers holding women back is to level the playing field with compensation and promotions. Tell job candidates when salary offers are flexible, since women are less likely than men to negotiate when it's unclear. List median salaries on job postings to give candidates more information. And base promotion decisions on data and facts about people's performance, not on anyone's self-nomination; the latter methods tend to favor men, since women who appear ambitious can face backlash.

Adapted from "How to Close the Gender Gap,"
by Colleen Ammerman and Boris Groysberg

Better Succession Planning

Rethink Your Process

Succession planning is complex and important to the ongoing success of your company. Many large companies don't pay enough attention to it, which comes with high costs. Flawed succession processes lead to excessive turnover among senior executives and destroy significant value for companies and investment portfolios. How significant? Badly managed CEO and C-suite transitions in the S&P 1500 wipe out close to $1 trillion a year in market value, according to research by a team representing Harvard Business School, Middle Tennessee State University, and the Tennessee Consolidated Retirement System. At the same time, the researchers estimate that with better succession planning, company valuations and investor returns would be 20% to 25% higher.

Is your executive team thinking about how to effectively transition to your company's future leaders?

Adapted from "The High Cost of Poor Succession Planning,"
by Claudio Fernández-Aráoz, Gregory Nagel, and Carrie Green

Keep Intuition and Analysis in Balance

One approach to decision-making is to build your expertise, then rely on your gut to make intuitive choices. Another popular approach is to analyze and base your decisions largely on data. The two methods have to be balanced: If you overvalue your gut, you might make decisions based on outdated, biased heuristics. If you overvalue data, you risk ignoring your inner compass, which can provide valuable insights from your experience.

How can you better balance your intuition and analytical sides to make good decisions?

Adapted from "Every Leader Needs to Navigate These 7 Tensions," by Jennifer Jordan, Michael Wade, and Elizabeth Teracino

Break Your Career-Limiting Habit

Change Your Frame

We all have a career-limiting habit, such as procrastinating or using our phones when we should be connecting with others. But people who overcome bad habits take control of the circumstances that feed them, according to research from Crucial Learning. One way to do this is to reframe your choices. Instead of saying "I won't do [your bad habit]," saying "I *can't* do that" can make you feel better able to resist it. Or instead of "I have to deal with this" about a tough situation, asking "Why do I *want* to deal with it?" can renew your motivation. Using different words and phrases can rewire how you think about challenges.

Adapted from "Trick Yourself into Breaking a Bad Habit,"
by Joseph Grenny

Develop Tomorrow's Skills Today

To prepare your workforce for the future, you'll need to use up-skilling and reskilling, but also *preskilling*—being able to future-proof talent and reinvent peoples' careers before we even know what tomorrow's jobs and in-demand skills will be. Five ways to preskill:

- Focus on potential, not just what people have done in the past

- Help employees understand how their interests, skills, and talents can be assets in the future

- Expand employees' skill sets—don't just optimize or strengthen existing abilities

- Develop middle managers' soft skills

- Invest in leaders who inspire, motivate, and promote collaboration

How can you use preskilling to develop your people?

Adapted from "5 Ways to Develop Talent for an Unpredictable Future," by Tomas Chamorro-Premuzic

What Successful People Do

Build Willpower

Why have you been so successful in reaching some of your goals, but not others? Even brilliant, highly accomplished people aren't great at understanding why they succeed or fail. But successful people do a few things differently, according to decades of research on achievement. One is building willpower. Taking on challenges that are truly difficult for you, and sticking with them, will strengthen your self-control "muscle" over time. Start with just one activity and make a plan for how you'll deal with obstacles ("If I have a craving for a snack, I will eat one piece of fresh fruit"). It will be difficult at first, but as your willpower grows, you can take on more challenges.

Adapted from "Nine Things Successful People Do
Differently," by Heidi Grant

Don't Assume You Know What Your Boss Expects

"The [employee] who passively assumes that [they] know what the boss expects is in for trouble. Of course, some [leaders] will spell out their expectations very explicitly and in great detail. But most do not. And although many corporations have systems that provide a basis for communicating expectations (such as formal planning processes . . . and performance appraisal reviews), these systems never work perfectly. . . . Ultimately, the burden falls on the [employee] to find out what the boss's expectations are. They can be both broad (such as what kinds of problems the boss wishes to be informed about and when) as well as very specific (such things as when a particular project should be completed and what kinds of information the boss needs in the interim). . . . Effective managers find ways to get that information."

Adapted from "Managing Your Boss,"
by John J. Gabarro and John P. Kotter

How to Make Your Employees Quit

Disregard Psychological Safety

Losing an employee hurts morale and productivity, and replacing people who leave is expensive. One mistake that can lead your people to quit is failing to create a culture of trust and empowerment. Employees who don't feel psychologically safe are less likely to take risks and engage in healthy conflict; those who do are more productive and innovative. So show your team that you're open to new ideas. Ask questions before posing answers and thank people for their input when they speak up. Consider all viewpoints when brainstorming and be clear that there's no wrong answer. And show humility: Own up to your faults and show employees it's OK to fail.

Adapted from "8 Things Leaders Do That Make
Employees Quit," by Jon Christiansen

Questions to Ask Yourself

Who Will Succeed Me?

Through the ups and downs of your career, regularly asking yourself a few questions can help you stay on track with your goals and priorities. One of those questions is: Have you identified some potential successors? In a sense, the goal of leadership is to train someone to one day take your place. Doing that requires delegating major tasks and giving stretch projects that help employees grow—which is also crucial because people who don't get growth opportunities are more likely to leave.

How are you challenging and preparing your most-skilled employees for the future?

Adapted from "What to Ask the Person in the Mirror,"
by Robert Steven Kaplan

The Persuasive Power of Authority

People are more likely to be convinced by someone who has deep expertise. That's why, if you need to be persuasive, an effective approach is to establish your knowledge about the topic at hand. In a meeting with a potential customer, for example, you might briefly mention your background and experience. Doing so early on gives people a sense of what's informing your perspective. Or, in a client dinner, you might tell an anecdote about solving a relevant problem or describe how you developed a skill. No matter how you do it, weave your expertise into the conversation organically—and avoid bragging.

Adapted from "Harnessing the Science of Persuasion,"
by Robert B. Cialdini

Make Empathy a Part of Your Company Culture

Empathy can improve collaboration and morale, while reducing employees' stress levels. To build it into your culture, think about whether it supports or clashes with your company norms. For example, if your culture rewards aggressive behavior, being more sensitive to other people's perspectives and feelings will be a hard sell. Next, consider how you can highlight the behaviors you want to encourage. When you see instances of empathy at work, recognize them publicly to help set an example. You should also identify "connector" employees, those who naturally encourage team cohesion, and recruit them to your cause. New ideals spread more easily when there are both top-down and bottom-up efforts.

Adapted from "Making Empathy Central to Your Company Culture," by Jamil Zaki

Your Employees Want to Learn New Skills

It's hard to build the workforce you'll need in the future when you're not sure what it will look like. What are the right skills? How will you find people with those skills? What do you do with people whose skills are obsolete? Do employees in disappearing jobs even know what's coming? Workers, though, don't share that sense of anxiety, according to a worldwide survey by researchers from Harvard Business School and Boston Consulting Group. They found that people are often more eager to embrace change and learn new skills than you might think.

What assumptions are you making about your employees' eagerness to learn new skills?

Adapted from "Your Workforce Is More Adaptable Than
You Think," by Joseph Fuller, Judith K. Wallenstein,
Manjari Raman, and Alice de Chalendar

Don't Stick to the Status Quo

New managers often fail, at least initially, because they have misconceptions about what it means to be a boss. One of these myths is that your primary challenge is to keep things running smoothly. But part of your job is to identify and initiate changes that will enhance your team's performance—which sometimes means challenging organizational processes or structures. If flawed systems, and the people responsible for them, are holding back your team, don't wait for someone else to fix the problem. Use your internal network and informal authority to advocate for the changes your employees need to succeed. Taking this broader view of your responsibilities will benefit you, your team, and your organization.

Adapted from "Becoming the Boss,"
by Linda A. Hill

Be Clearer About the Strategic Changes You Want

"Too many followers tasked with delivering strategic change report that their leaders weren't clear enough about what they wanted the change to achieve or about what it would entail. It seems the reasons for this are twofold: Leaders too often express what they want in terms not of *outcomes*, but of *tasks*, and they rarely, if ever, make clear the full *extent* of the change they are asking for."

When you're leading strategic initiatives, how could you be clearer about your expectations?

———————————

Adapted from "How to Communicate Clearly During Organizational Change," by Elsbeth Johnson

Be a Visionary Leader— Right Now

Maybe you think a visionary leader has to be a CEO, or at least a high-level manager. But visionary leadership is important if you're a middle or frontline manager too, since you play a key role in carrying out strategic change at any level. Your ability to inspire your team and create strategic alignment—a shared understanding of and commitment to the larger strategy—is vitally important to supporting and executing the company's long-term plans.

What steps can you take to build your visionary capacity?

Adapted from "Why Visionary Leadership Fails,"
by Nufer Yasin Ates, Murat Tarakci, Jeanine P. Porck,
Daan van Knippenberg, and Patrick Groenen

What to Learn Next

Something You're Passionate About

Great leaders never stop learning, but how do you know what skill you should work on next? One approach is to choose something that you're especially excited to learn. Across your career there will be any number of things to study, so if one seems especially interesting, start there. For example, if you've identified two skills to hone this year—process architecture and providing clearer direction—and the former appeals to you more, find a training course on it. But remember that just because a certain topic is less exciting doesn't mean it isn't important; you can motivate yourself to study it by picturing how it will help your career or team.

Adapted from "How to Decide What Skill to Work On Next,"
by Erika Andersen

Use Seven-Year Periods to Weather Change

To deal with career transitions better, try dividing your life into seven-year periods. Think about the highlights and learnings of each era, including who you were when each period started and ended. Also consider each era's challenges and setbacks, and how they affected your identity. Framing your life this way can impose a rhythm: You're at a beginning, in a middle, or nearing an end. It can also help you weather change more effectively, since you'll sense the arc of jobs, life phases, or relationships. Then when significant shifts happen, your mental model can provide perspective and context to keep you grounded.

What are the highlights and learnings of your seven-year periods so far?

Adapted from "Learn to Get Better at Transitions,"
by Avivah Wittenberg-Cox

Take Criticism Like a Leader

As a leader, you need to know how to take criticism well. One strategy is to brainstorm responses in advance, so you'll have something ready to say if you need it. Keep it simple: "Thank you for sharing your point of view. I'd like to consider it more and get back to you." Another good strategy is to remember that criticism may be aimed at your role rather than at you personally. If you're the head of product, you might feel at odds with the head of sales due to differing priorities—but those tensions may exist no matter who holds the role. Distancing yourself from criticism this way can help you think through what was said, and what the feedback is really about.

Adapted from "How to Take Criticism Well,"
by Sabina Nawaz

Don't Hold Your Mentees Back

In a mentoring relationship, be wary of misusing your power. If you cross any lines, even unintentionally, there could be negative career consequences for both you and your mentee. Watch out for:

- Taking credit for your mentees' ideas or usurping lead position on their projects

- Insisting that your mentees advance your projects rather than allowing them to develop their own work

- Tethering your mentee to your timeline, slowing their progress

- Discouraging your mentees from seeking other mentors, which may stroke your ego but isolate them from broader learning and recognition

- Allowing mentees to repeat common self-destructive mistakes without reining them in

---

Adapted from "6 Things Every Mentor Should Do,"
by Vineet Chopra and Sanjay Saint

Clarify Tricky Problems with One Question

Your job as a leader is filled with hard decisions. It's natural to want to think about issues from multiple angles. That means, though, that you risk getting bogged down in the potential fallout of each course of action; it can be paralyzing to feel that every option has a downside. When you're in this position, one simple question can help you clarify your thinking: What's best for the organization? Especially when you're confronting tough decisions about employees, stepping back and remembering the bigger picture can guide your choices.

When could taking a broader perspective help you make better decisions?

Adapted from "The Leap to Leader,"
by Adam Bryant

Your Life Story Is Part of Your Authenticity

Knowing who you are and where you come from is part of being authentic. To reflect on your own authenticity, think about your personal story, including the people and events that have given meaning to your life. Consider both the good (which may include parents and mentors, wins and promotions) and the bad (micro-managers and narcissists, illnesses and job losses). Authentic leaders often find motivation in hardships and reframe tragic events to rise above their challenges and discover their passion to lead.

What people and experiences have had the greatest impact on your life and leadership?

Adapted from "Discovering Your Authentic Leadership,"
by Bill George, Peter Sims, Andrew N. McLean, and Diana Mayer

How to Lose Well

Share the Pain

As a leader, you're focused on winning. But no one is successful all the time; you need to learn to lose with grace. One approach is to make space for your, and others', negative feelings. Losing can involve heartbreak, frustration, and sorrow—across a team or an entire organization. So encourage people to talk about how they're feeling, and even share stories of past professional failures to help one another gain perspective.

When people feel free to not excel at all times, it helps create psychological safety, which boosts collaboration, innovation, and productivity. Hard times bring people together; don't overlook the value in that dynamic.

Adapted from "Good Leaders Lose with Grace,"
by Tim Leberecht

Clarify Your Meeting's Decision-Making Process

When there's confusion around how, or by whom, the final call will be made, meetings can get tense. So start your meetings by explaining the ground rules. You might tell the group there will be 30 minutes of discussion and then a vote, and if there is no resolution the issue will be brought to an executive. Or, if an executive is in the room, they might make the decision right then. Explain the finer points too: Does anyone have veto power? Does the group vote determine the final decision, but a two-thirds majority is needed? Whatever the process, explain it clearly before you dive in.

Adapted from "A Good Meeting Needs a Clear Decision-Making Process," by Bob Frisch and Cary Greene

To Inspire, Get Centered

"Inspiring leaders are those who use their unique combination of strengths to motivate individuals and teams to take on bold missions—and hold them accountable for results. And they unlock higher performance through empowerment, not command and control. . . . Although we found that many different attributes help leaders inspire people . . . there is one trait that our [research] indicated matters more than any other: centeredness. This is a state of mindfulness that enables leaders to remain calm under stress, empathize, listen deeply, and remain present."

How do you maintain your centeredness even when work gets hectic?

Adapted from "How to Be an Inspiring Leader,"
by Eric Garton

Give People Time to Process Change

When leaders announce change initiatives, too often they try to talk employees out of the doubt or skepticism they're feeling, assuming people will get on board eventually. But you've already had weeks or months to think about the change; your employees are hearing about it for the first time. Of course, they may ask questions or worry about the impact to their jobs. Give people time to experience these feelings. Ask about their concerns without being dismissive and talk through what the change means for them. Don't think of it as "resistance"—helping your people feel heard and supported is how you'll build the buy-in your change needs to succeed.

Adapted from "Change Is Hard. Here's How to Make It
Less Painful," by Erika Andersen

Know When to Stop Talking and Start Listening

You have to talk a lot when you're a leader. You want people to have the guidance and direction they need, but eventually talking a lot can turn into dominating conversations and others' perspectives. To rein yourself in, listen as much as you speak. When someone raises a question in a meeting, invite several others to weigh in before you—that way everyone is included and feels that their input is valued. You can also schedule regular one-on-one sessions with your team members to encourage open communication. Ask employees about their wants, needs, and concerns—and then hush. You may be surprised how much you learn when you're saying nothing.

Adapted from "Don't Be the Boss Who Talks Too Much," by Hjalmar Gislason

Questions to Ask Yourself

Am I Staying True to Who I Am?

Through the ups and downs of your career, regularly asking yourself a few questions can help you stay on track with your goals and priorities. One of those questions is: Does your leadership style reflect who you really are? While you can model your style on other leaders you admire, ultimately it must be unique and authentic to you. And as you assume more-senior positions, there are other considerations to be wary of, such as whether you're assertive enough or whether you hesitate to share tough feedback because you don't want your team to look bad.

How well does your leadership style reflect your skills, values, and personality?

———————————

Adapted from "What to Ask the Person in the Mirror,"
by Robert Steven Kaplan

How to Develop Open-Mindedness

Open-mindedness at work—about new products, strategies, business models, and more—is one key to success. There are many ways to develop this trait. A few ideas:

- **Travel.** As you encounter different ways of living, your brain will get better at accepting new approaches and ideas.

- **Read fiction.** Novels can train your brain to be curious about others' experiences, perspectives, and opinions.

- **Try mindfulness meditation.** A regular mindfulness practice has been shown to help people be willing to revise their ideas.

- **Start sentences with "I could be wrong, but…"** This phrase conveys your openness—and your willingness to change your mind.

Adapted from "A New Way to Become More Open-Minded,"
by Shane Snow

Analyze Your Failures and Successes Together

It's natural to analyze a failure's root causes and look for patterns. But some patterns are common to your successes, too. That's why you should examine failures and successes together— to see what mitigation strategies will actually help. For example, say some of your employees fell short on a project and weren't using the team's workflow management tool. You may think the answer is simple: Use the tool more. But what if the successful employees weren't using it much either? Before you invest in new solutions, tools, and trainings, take a closer look at what really caused a failure.

Adapted from "Don't Learn the Wrong Lessons from Failure,"
by Emre Soyer and Robin M. Hogarth

Don't Mistake Quiet for Lack of Passion

Employees who display passion—being visibly excited, chatting eagerly with colleagues—receive more support from managers and are more likely to be seen as high potentials. But if you assume quieter employees are less passionate about work, you devalue their contributions. People show enthusiasm in many ways, and some are harder to observe, such as being careful and thorough, dedicating extra time to a project, and becoming deeply immersed in key details. So instead of using outsize displays of emotion as a proxy for commitment, focus on the quality of people's work. Just because some employees express themselves differently than others doesn't mean they care any less.

Adapted from "Stop Assuming Introverts Aren't Passionate About Work," by Kai Krautter, Anabel Büchner, and Jon M. Jachimowicz

Your Mood Drives Business Results

When you're the leader, your mood is contagious, spreading quickly and inexorably throughout the business, according to research on neurology, psychology, and leadership styles. Because your mood and accompanying behaviors are such potent drivers of success, your premier task is emotional leadership. You need to make sure that not only are you regularly in an optimistic, authentic, high-energy mood, but also that, through your chosen actions, your followers feel and act that way, too. Managing for financial results, then, begins with managing your inner life so that the right emotional and behavioral chain reaction occurs.

How can you get better at managing your inner life this week, this month, this year?

Adapted from "Primal Leadership: The Hidden Driver of Great Performance," by Daniel Goleman, Richard E. Boyatzis, and Annie McKee

When Work Is Overwhelming

Change Your Behavior

When you have too much to do, you may feel anxious any time you're not working. But a huge to-do list doesn't have to overwhelm you. One strategy for managing stress is to act more relaxed about it. Part of our psychology is that changing your behavior can change your emotions in turn. Ask "If I were more relaxed about my workload, how would I act?" For example, maybe a less-stressed you would step away from work to eat lunch and unwind for a few minutes, even if that feels impossible. Identify a few possible changes—and make them. Acting calmer about work can actually help you *be* calmer about it.

Adapted from "5 Things to Do When You Feel Overwhelmed
by Your Workload," by Alice Boyes

To Create Better Agendas, Ask Questions

You know your meetings need structure to stay focused, but it's not always obvious what makes a great agenda. Instead of listing the discussion topics as bullet points, try using questions that the group will answer together. For example, "Budget problems" could become "How will we reduce spending by $100K this year?" and "Customer response times" could become "How can we reduce customer response times by 25%?" Questions will keep you focused on the desired outcomes, and help you assess the invite list: Whose expertise is needed to answer a certain question? Using questions to set your agenda will also help you know when a meeting is done—when everything has been answered.

Adapted from "How to Create the Perfect Meeting Agenda," by Steven G. Rogelberg

Write So It Sounds Like a Human Wrote It

Clear, engaging writing keeps people coming back for more; stiff, aloof text does the opposite. So whatever you're drafting, aim to sound like a human, not a business—or an AI chatbot. How? Use the first person whenever you can since it feels personal and inviting ("I did . . ." or "We accomplished . . . ," not "The company achieved . . ."). Don't be afraid to start sentences with imperatives ("Get," "Join," "Download") or conjunctions ("Or," "And," "But"), since that's how we talk in real life. And read your message aloud to weed out business-speak. If something sounds awkward to you, it'll sound awkward to readers.

Adapted from "Writing About Business (Without Being a Bore)," by Mike Reed

Make It Safer to Speak Up

Psychological safety helps teams operate at their highest level. To build it on your team, start with the basics: establishing clear norms and expectations, encouraging open communication, actively listening to employees, and showing appreciation and humility when people express their ideas and concerns. Then go beyond the basics. One way is by setting the stage for people to speak up. Explain why you need everyone's point of view, why their input matters, and how it will affect the outcomes of the work. Also, discuss the downsides of not getting the group's varied perspectives, such as lower collective creativity. For most people, staying quiet feels safe so you have to work to override that instinct.

Adapted from "What Is Psychological Safety?," by Amy Gallo

What's Your Leadership Style?

Coaching

Your personal leadership style has a powerful impact on your organization. One type of leadership that has positive effects on an organization's working environment and results is the coaching style. Coaching leaders help employees identify their unique strengths and weaknesses and tie them to their personal and career aspirations. They encourage employees to establish long-term development goals, give plenty of feedback, and assign challenging projects for growth. This approach works well when employees are already aware of their weaknesses and realize how cultivating new skills can help them advance; it makes less sense when people are resistant to changing their ways. As you lead, consider what style a situation calls for, and whether your current approach is working well or may need adjusting.

Adapted from "Leadership That Gets Results,"
by Daniel Goleman

Present Data Clearly

Having data doesn't guarantee your presentation will be effective; you need to label the data so it's easily understood. Use precise language to identify chart elements such as axes, bars, and lines. Avoid vague labels and abbreviations that aren't obvious, and don't assume people will remember labels from previous slides. You should also drop generic titles in favor of specific, memorable ones. Instead of "Millennial Preferences," try "Millennials Prefer Mobile" to underline the takeaway. And highlight aha zones in the data by circling or shading it, as well as calling it out verbally.

Adapted from "Present Your Data Like a Pro,"
by Joel Schwartzberg

Build Your Emotional Courage

Part of your role as a leader is doing things that feel uncomfortable, such as raising a tough issue with an employee. To improve how you deal with uncomfortable situations, build your emotional courage. Think of a leadership skill you want to improve—giving feedback, listening, being direct—and hone that skill in a low-risk situation. For example, if there's a mistake on your phone bill, practice being direct by calling customer service and stating the problem succinctly and clearly. Notice how you *want* to react—Get angry? Backpedal?—and resist those impulses. Keep practicing until you can respond the way you'd like to.

Adapted from "To Develop Leadership Skills, Practice in a Low-Risk Environment," by Peter Bregman

Develop Your Learning Agility

Make Time for Reflection

If you rely on the same assumptions and behavioral repertoires you've used for years as a leader, you are prone to stagnate, underperform, or derail, according to research from Korn Ferry. The solution is to develop learning agility, the capacity for rapid, continuous learning. One method to keep growing is to make time for reflection. Regularly reflecting on your work experiences boosts your learning significantly, according to research from multiple universities. To ensure continuous progress, get into the habit of asking yourself questions like "What have I learned from this experience?" and "What turned out differently than I expected?" When you demonstrate and encourage reflection, you'll learn more yourself—and encourage the same in your team.

Adapted from "4 Ways to Become a Better Learner,"
by Monique Valcour

Are Your Managers Strategically Aligned?

As a leader, you may think your company's managers are aligned around the organization's strategy. But are you sure? Lots of senior leaders take it for granted that middle and frontline managers are strategically aligned—rather than confirming that assumption and, when necessary, taking the time to get everyone on board. Alignment isn't a one-time goal, it's a continuous dialogue about what's important and prioritized. Managers will only take ownership of the strategy if they're convinced of its value.

How are you creating strategic alignment among your company's managers?

Adapted from "Why Visionary Leadership Fails," by Nufer Yasin Ates, Murat Tarakci, Jeanine P. Porck, Daan van Knippenberg, and Patrick Groenen

You Don't Make Products, You Serve Customers

"The entire corporation must be viewed as a customer-creating and customer-satisfying organism. Management must think of itself not as producing products but as providing customer-creating value satisfactions. It must push this idea (and everything it means and requires) into every nook and cranny of the organization. It has to do this continuously and with the kind of flair that excites and stimulates the people in it. Otherwise, the company will be merely a series of pigeonholed parts, with no consolidating sense of purpose or direction. . . . The organization must learn to think of itself not as producing goods or services but as *buying customers,* as doing the things that will make people *want* to do business with it."

Adapted from "Marketing Myopia,"
by Theodore Levitt

Don't Be a Victim of Your Success

Invite Dissent

To keep performing at your best, you must overcome the barriers that accompany your success. One barrier is growing accustomed to not being questioned or challenged. Successful leaders are often surrounded by people who won't dispute their views. But if you get used to continual agreement—and never hear dissenting points of view—you may start deluding yourself about your abilities. And then if peers or more-senior leaders think your solution to a problem isn't robust enough or hasn't considered all the factors, you may struggle to defend your position.

How do you seek out multiple, diverse perspectives on problems and potential solutions?

Adapted from "Want to Change the World? Don't Let Your Own Success Get in the Way," by Rosabeth Moss Kanter

Tell Your Team to Take a Vacation

Taking time off is good for productivity, so if your employees aren't using all their paid vacation days, encourage them to do so. Start by modeling what you want to see: Go on vacation, be open about it—and don't send email while you're away. You can also change expectations about time off: Some employees may want a week away, but others may prefer shorter breaks, such as an occasional day or afternoon. Finally, make vacation a team effort by asking employees to share responsibilities and cover for each other. The easier it is for people to use their days off, the more they will.

Adapted from "Managers, Encourage Your Team to Take Time Off," by Sabina Nawaz

How to Make Your Employees Quit

Be Too Safe

Losing an employee hurts morale and productivity, and replacing people who leave is expensive. One mistake that can lead your people to quit is creating a work environment that is a little *too* safe. A moderate level of pressure helps employees perform; too little pressure, though, leads people to feel less productive, less purposeful, and less loyal. So, cultivate an environment of psychological safety, but allow for a healthy amount of friction on your team. Provide regular feedback—positive and negative—to give employees something to work toward. Use frequent, pointed coaching to identify areas for improvement. And remind people of how their roles contribute to the larger organization, which keeps them focused on the bigger picture.

Adapted from "8 Things Leaders Do That Make Employees Quit," by Jon Christiansen

Support Extroverts in Hybrid Settings

You know that introverts and extroverts differ in work styles, communication preferences, and social needs. So how do you support your extrovert employees in hybrid work arrangements? If they aren't feeling connected, meet with them regularly (face-to-face or on video) to catch up and discuss their work. In the office, foster watercooler moments to strengthen relationships spontaneously. Hold optional team events, such as hybrid lunches or happy hours, to help employees build camaraderie, morale, and trust. And in meetings, use virtual breakout groups so that extroverts can talk out their ideas. When your extroverts are working outside the office, or with colleagues who are, they need social connection more than ever.

Adapted from "Managing Introverts and Extroverts in the Hybrid Workplace," by Erica Dhawan

Transition to Senior Leadership

Become a Diplomat

When you shift from leading a function to leading an enterprise, you must navigate a tricky set of changes in your leadership focus and skills. One change is becoming a diplomat. In your prior roles, you focused on leading your team to defeat competitors. Now you'll also spend time addressing the concerns and (sometimes competing) priorities of other top leaders, their business units, and the people above you—all the way up to the board. You'll need a new mindset about negotiation, persuasion, and alliance building—looking for where interests can or do align and understanding how decisions are made in different organizations. The role of a diplomat is to think long-term and collaboratively.

Adapted from "How Managers Become Leaders,"
by Michael D. Watkins

Does Your Career Support Your Purpose?

Early in our careers, our choices are often influenced by outside factors, from bosses' expectations to societal ideas of success. As you gain experience, it's important to consider what *you* find meaningful. To take stock of where you are and where you want to go, ask yourself: Are you pursuing your purpose? Think about what excites you, what fulfills you, and what you're curious about. Then consider how your career path supports those factors. If the answer is "not very well," look for ways to shift your current responsibilities to better align with your desired direction. Making even small changes now can lead to more satisfaction later.

Adapted from "6 Questions to Ask at the Midpoint of
Your Career," by Rebecca Knight

When Your Team's Vibe Is Off

Reset Its Mandate and Goals

If your team is feeling stuck or stale, it could be because employees have lost sight of their purpose and the goals they're working toward. Whether the malaise is due to external factors or internal ones (or both), sometimes your team's mandate and goals need a refresh. Discussing a few questions as a group can help:

1. What external trends do we need to adapt to?

2. How do shifts in company strategy affect us?

3. How is our value in the company evolving?

4. How will we build on our prior results?

5. What external factors affect our goals?

6. How can we improve our success metrics?

Use the answers to realign your team around a fresh sense of purpose.

Adapted from "20 Questions to Ask When Your Team's
Vibe Is Off," by Liane Davey

The Mental Shifts of Leadership

"[There are] mental shifts needed to become a leader and to handle the challenges you'll encounter in your new role. The process involves identifying and communicating your core values and learning how to approach tough decisions. It requires setting the bar for your team's performance and learning to compartmentalize so that you can find the right pace for yourself. And it requires expanding your self-awareness and paying attention to the stories you tell yourself about your experiences—your successes and failures, your bad times and good ones—when you contemplate the arc of your career and life."

What kinds of mental shifts have you had to make about work or yourself as a leader?

Adapted from "The Leap to Leader,"
by Adam Bryant

The Power of Personal Storytelling

The more powerful you are, the more you need empathy, since it can stave off the self-absorption that power can cause. To build empathy, you have a few options. One is to use storytelling to make things personal. Having your employees share stories about their work and challenges can help people (including you) transcend their own perspectives. Find ways for workers at all levels to learn more about one another's roles and contributions; you may want to share your own point of view as well. Whether through larger meetings or smaller group discussions, hearing from colleagues can build trust and empathy, and inspire you to better support your employees.

Adapted from "Don't Let Power Corrupt You,"
by Julie Battilana and Tiziana Casciaro

Get Better at Saying No

You have far more work than you can actually do; you need to say no to things that aren't in line with your goals and priorities. Since turning people down can be uncomfortable, practice saying no politely and gracefully. For example, if a colleague asks you to do something that conflicts with your top objectives, try "This might be a great growth opportunity for someone. I'm happy to connect you with Kei, who's looking to develop in that area." If you're asked to join a project that you don't have time for, say "Thanks, but I have to decline. My schedule is at capacity." Practice can help you set boundaries around the areas that need your attention the most.

Adapted from "9 Ways to Say No to Busywork and Unrealistic Deadlines," by Elizabeth Grace Saunders

Questions to Ask Yourself

Am I Monitoring Wider Business Changes?

Through the ups and downs of your career, regularly asking yourself a few questions can help you stay on track with your goals and priorities. One of those questions is: Are you attuned to changes in the business environment? As customers' needs evolve, your company grows, or new products emerge, how you run your business has to change too. That change process can be painful, as it can involve letting people go, reorganizing jobs or functions, or even adjusting your own leadership style. But the alternative is failing to change with the times, which can be deadly.

How do you make sure that the ways you run your business remain flexible?

Adapted from "What to Ask the Person in the Mirror,"
by Robert Steven Kaplan

When Work Is Overwhelming

Track Your Time

When you have too much to do, you may feel anxious any time you're not working. But a huge to-do list doesn't have to overwhelm you. One strategy for managing stress is to track your time. Keep a record of your work for a week, noting the hours spent on each task. Then look for patterns, including things you spend too much time on. Having an accurate, rather than stress-induced, view of your days can help you think critically about where you might cut back. Also look for time wasters like scrolling headlines, and limit them to when you're in between tasks, so you don't disrupt your productivity.

Adapted from "5 Things to Do When You Feel Overwhelmed by Your Workload," by Alice Boyes

Micromanagers Don't Realize How Damaging They Are

Effective managers establish themselves as resources for team members; they check *in* while never seeming to check *up* on people. Micromanagers do the opposite—and make four kinds of mistakes. First, they don't allow autonomy in how people do their jobs. Second, they frequently ask people about their progress without providing any real help. Third, they're quick to assign personal blame when problems arise—which can lead people to hide issues. Fourth, they tend to hoard information to use as a weapon. If any of these behaviors sound familiar, think about the negative effects you've having on your team, and how changing your ways could better support your employees' success.

Adapted from "The Power of Small Wins,"
by Teresa M. Amabile and Steven J. Kramer

An Underused Tool

Notes of Appreciation

When you want to show someone—employees, peers, even bosses—that you appreciate their work, don't overlook the power of a simple note. Whether it's handwritten or emailed, the key is to be specific about why you find their contributions important. For example, you might say, "You bring pragmatism to our conversations, which moves us from theory to action," or "You view all situations with empathy, helping us make more caring decisions." These notes are potent ways to highlight people's strengths, and they're a good way for you to reflect on what you value in others. Proactively writing them also shows that you care and will go out of your way to show it.

Adapted from "Notes of Appreciation Can Boost Individual and Team Morale," by Whitney Johnson and Amy Humble

Better Succession Planning

Look Inside Your Company

Succession planning is complex and important to the ongoing success of your company. If your company is looking for a new CEO, should you hire an internal candidate who knows the organization or an external one who can bring an outsider's perspective? It depends, according to studies from Harvard Business School and the Wharton School. Companies that are doing poorly can benefit greatly from an outsider who shakes things up. At companies already doing well, however, outsider CEOs often destroy massive value—and in addition, they tend to be paid more, perform worse, and have higher exit rates. So unless you're in need of a major turnaround or culture change, your company may be better off promoting someone from within.

Adapted from "The High Cost of Poor Succession Planning,"
by Claudio Fernández-Aráoz, Gregory Nagel, and Carrie Green

Break Your Career-Limiting Habit

Train Yourself

We all have a career-limiting habit, such as procrastinating or using our phones when we should be connecting with others. But people who overcome bad habits take control of the circumstances that feed them, according to research from Crucial Learning. One way to do this is to train yourself in the area you want to improve. Create small, structured opportunities to practice a new habit or focus. If you want to develop your interpersonal skills, identify one technique to try each week and one situation to practice it in. By taking small, regular steps, you'll increase your sense of competence and boost your motivation to continue.

Adapted from "Trick Yourself into Breaking a Bad Habit,"
by Joseph Grenny

Understand Employees' Job Satisfaction

Part of your role as a leader is making sure your employees have what they need to thrive. Yet research from Gallup found that 51% of employees who quit say no one, including their boss, asked about their job satisfaction before they left. To find out how people are really doing, ask a few questions:

1. How would you like to grow here?

2. Do you feel a sense of purpose in your job?

3. What do you need from me to do your best work?

4. What is the company not doing that it should do?

5. Are you able to do what you do best every day?

Use the answers to identify problems you can solve, and to look for growth opportunities for your people.

Adapted from "5 Questions Every Manager Needs to Ask Their Direct Reports," by Susan Peppercorn

Your Leadership Voice

Built on Connection

Cultivating your leadership voice requires building the capacity to respond authentically, constructively, and effectively, no matter the situation or audience. One aspect of your voice is connection. As your purview expands, staying close to all your colleagues, networks, and teams becomes more difficult. Find ways to develop and maintain bonds with people, whether by telling stories about your work's impact, expressing gratitude for others' efforts, or making time to build rapport in a conversation or a meeting. When you do, you'll show that you truly care about others and their success.

How do you use your voice of connection to strengthen your work relationships?

Adapted from "You Don't Just Need One Leadership Voice—
You Need Many," by Amy Jen Su

What to Learn Next

Something You'll Excel At

Great leaders never stop learning, but how do you know what skill you should work on next? One approach is to choose something that you could excel at. Consider the skills you currently have, and then brainstorm some related, parallel, or complementary abilities that you might have an innate talent for. For example, if you're especially organized and detail-oriented, honing your knowledge about complex project management could make sense; if you aren't great at doing research, though, getting better at sourcing materials might not be your best choice. And if you need help in thinking through what you're best at, ask trusted colleagues for feedback on what they see as your top strengths.

Adapted from "How to Decide What Skill to Work On Next,"
by Erika Andersen

When You Reach an Inflection Point, Pause to Reflect

"Points of inflection—life's *what now?* moments—emerge frequently across our professional and personal lives. They can arise from difficulty, like when we lose a job unexpectedly or are forced to deal with a chronic illness, or . . . in the wake of exciting new opportunities. Whatever the catalyst, points of transition can feel threatening, especially when our identity and self-direction are called into question. . . . Developing a practice of pausing to regulate, resource, and reorient before we respond can counteract the threat response and help us to be more curious and creative in the face of *what now?* moments, even when we're not sure what comes next."

Adapted from "You've Reached an Inflection Point in Your Career. What Now?," by Joan P. Ball and Julia Beck

Focusing as a Leader

On Yourself

One of your primary tasks as a leader is to direct attention. To do that, first learn to focus your own attention, in three broad ways: on yourself, on others, and on the wider world. Focusing on yourself means having the self-awareness to monitor your internal signals and to combine your experiences across time into a coherent view of yourself. It also means having the self-control to put your attention where you want it and keep it there amid distractions. Leaders who can do these tasks will be better in touch with their authentic selves, which helps them keep pursuing goals even in the face of setbacks.

Adapted from "The Focused Leader,"
by Daniel Goleman

Your Big Project Needs Three Kinds of Employees

When you're staffing a high-profile project, you need more than just high performers. Look for employees who:

- **Are comfortable with uncertainty.** Seek out individuals who will remain curious and focused even when the project is far from the end goal.

- **Create structure within chaos and take action.** Recruit workers who can drive a team forward even when circumstances change.

- **Connect and execute.** Find employees who can see links between different information and ideas, and then create something tangible from the results.

With these people on board, your team will be well positioned to capture new opportunities.

Adapted from "If Your Innovation Effort Isn't Working, Look at Who's on the Team," by Nathan Furr, Kyle Nel, and Thomas Zoëga Ramsøy

Make Everyone Feel Welcome at Casual Networking Events

Informal events can be useful ways to connect, share information, and even make decisions. But they can also exclude some team members, even unintentionally, so work to ensure everyone feels welcome. Start by learning your employees' preferences about social gatherings, including dietary restrictions and group activities. For example, avoid centering every event around alcohol, so people who don't drink aren't excluded, and plan some gatherings during the day or over lunch, so people who can't stay late don't miss out. And pay attention to who's showing up; if certain employees don't attend often, check in and make sure they know they're invited.

Adapted from "How Managers Can Make Casual Networking Events More Inclusive," by Ruchika Tulshyan

Short Naps, Big Rewards

"[An] overlooked tool for getting more rest is napping. Too often, leaders view nap breaks as time spent loafing instead of working. However, research clearly indicates that dozing for even 20 minutes can lead to meaningful restoration that improves the quality of work. A brief nap can speed up cognitive processing, decrease errors, and increase stamina for sustained attention to difficult tasks later in the day. One study [from the University of Düsseldorf] found that as little as eight minutes of sleep during the day was enough to significantly improve memory."

Adapted from "Sleep Well, Lead Better,"
by Christopher M. Barnes

To Help Women Get Ahead

Get Them to Stay

As a leader, you know that women are still dramatically under-represented in positions of power: Few *Fortune* 500 companies are led by women, and even fewer by women of color. One way to reduce the barriers holding women back is to lower turnover among them. If women think it's nearly impossible to grow and advance, they will leave. Reward and promote people for their results, not how many hours they work. Don't penalize mothers, women who prioritize work-life balance, or those who prefer remote/flexible work; women who don't feel treated fairly won't stick around. Having more women in the upper ranks, however, shows employees that progression is possible—and it also decreases sexual harassment, another drain on retention.

Adapted from "How to Close the Gender Gap,"
by Colleen Ammerman and Boris Groysberg

Prepare to Speak Up in Meetings

Contributing your ideas in meetings increases your visibility at work, but it doesn't come naturally to everyone. If you struggle to offer your thoughts on the spot, try asking a simple question before the meeting: "Why me?" Consider the topic and attendees and think about what you can offer that others can't. Why do you care about the topic, your organization, your role? What unique expertise or insights do you have for the meeting's discussion? What concerns or warnings are you well positioned to raise? Answering "Why me?" connects to your sense of purpose and can build your confidence, because your credibility comes from your experience, commitment, and passion.

Adapted from "How to Speak Up in a Meeting, and
When to Hold Back," by Allison Shapira

What Trade-Offs Are You Willing to Make?

All careers involve trade-offs. As your skill set and experience open up more options, it's worth thinking about which compromises still feel worthwhile—and which don't. For example, maybe your children are grown, so now you want to focus more on your career. Or maybe you're tired of lacking time for hobbies and travel, and you want to pursue those activities. Let your values and priorities guide this process. Because they evolve over time, you'll want to reflect on these dynamics regularly—once a year, perhaps, or whatever interval seems right for you. There are no wrong choices; just be intentional about aligning your goals with the sacrifices you're making.

Adapted from "6 Questions to Ask at the Midpoint of Your Career," by Rebecca Knight

As Your Importance Grows, So Does Your Ego

You acquire more power as you rise in rank. And being more powerful means people want to please you, whether by listening more attentively, agreeing with you, or laughing at your jokes. Those things may feel good, but if your ego gets too big, it will warp your perspective and values. Breaking free of that dynamic isn't easy—it takes selflessness, reflection, and courage—but it's important and challenging work.

How do you keep your ego in check?

Adapted from "Ego Is the Enemy of Good Leadership,"
by Rasmus Hougaard and Jacqueline Carter

New Leaders, Explain Yourself

When you transition into leadership, you need to show employees, bosses, and peers what you bring to the table. One group of questions you'll face are about you as a professional—your background, competencies, experience, and leadership approach. People want to know whether you can do the job, and whether you'll help them do theirs better or just get in the way. It's unlikely that anyone is purposefully trying to undermine you; you're being compared with your role's previous holder, since people want to know what to expect. By thinking through what matters to and worries different groups, you can tailor your approach to start these new relationships effectively.

Adapted from "Stepping into a Leadership Role? Be Ready to Tell Your Story," by David Sluss

Develop a Strategy for Your Career

Invest Your Time

To ensure a meaningful career, create a long-term strategy for it. One step is to invest your time wisely. Time is the currency of our lives, and how we spend it speaks volumes about what we think is important. Make a simple pie chart of how you've spent your time over the past couple of months; use categories such as work, family, community, health, or just downtime. Are you devoting enough of yourself to things that bring lasting satisfaction? Are you devoting too much to things that don't? Use your chart to think about whether fulfilling your purpose requires you to reallocate your hours; you don't have an infinite supply of them.

Adapted from "Developing a Strategy for a Life of Meaningful Labor," by Brian Fetherstonhaugh

Are You Doing Enough to Retain Your Best Employees?

When retention issues crop up, it's easy to blame anyone but yourself. But think carefully about why your employees are leaving and consider whether—and how—you might be contributing to the problem. Then find out more. For instance, having supportive, frank discussions about job satisfaction, in which you ask employees to share both good and bad feedback, can help you keep tabs on how people feel about their jobs (and you). You might hear some uncomfortable truths, but don't get defensive. Be open to listening and to adjusting how you manage based on what people say. If you signal to employees that you're willing to make meaningful changes, they may feel more inclined to stay.

Adapted from "Don't Let Lazy Managers Drive Away Your Top Performers," by Mark C. Bolino and Anthony C. Klotz

What Successful People Do

Replace Bad Habits with Better Ones

Why have you been so successful in reaching some of your goals, but not others? Even brilliant, highly accomplished people aren't great at understanding why they succeed or fail. But successful people do a few things differently, according to decades of research on achievement. One is to shift your focus from what you *won't* do to what you *will* do. Make a plan to replace bad habits and unproductive behaviors with better ones: For example, "If I start to feel angry, I will take three deep breaths to calm down." By using deep breathing as a replacement for giving in to your anger, the bad habit will get worn away over time until it disappears completely.

Adapted from "Nine Things Successful People Do
Differently," by Heidi Grant

Don't Choke Under Pressure

When a talented leader bombs a job interview or botches a presentation, often it's because they're too in their head. They panic about the situation and its consequences and start overthinking what comes naturally to them. To stay cool when the pressure is on, don't dwell on what you're about to do. Spend the five minutes before your big meeting doing a crossword puzzle or thinking about your upcoming vacation—not going over every detail of your presentation. If you're still overthinking, try repeating a simple mantra, focusing on your talk's three key points, or (quietly) singing a song. The goal is to use up extra cognitive horsepower that your brain could turn against you.

Adapted from "Why Talented People Fail Under Pressure," by Sian Beilock

Great Persuaders
Read the Room

"Effective persuaders have a strong and accurate sense of their audience's emotional state, and they adjust the tone of their arguments accordingly. Sometimes that means coming on strong, with forceful points. Other times, a whisper may be all that is required. The idea is that whatever your position, you match your emotional fervor to your audience's ability to receive the message."

Adapted from "The Necessary Art of Persuasion,"
by Jay A. Conger

When Being Powerful Makes It Harder to Lead

"People at the top tend to become less attentive to [employees]. . . . Not 'seeing' the people you lead diminishes effectiveness all around. You can't lead colleagues you don't understand—and people aren't motivated or able to contribute their best efforts if they perceive that you are disconnected from and uninterested in them. You might be able to push through in the short term, but eventually their performance will suffer and your leadership may be called into question. To effectively exercise power while avoiding its pitfalls, leaders must cultivate humility as an antidote to hubris and empathy as an antidote to self-focus."

Adapted from "Don't Let Power Corrupt You,"
by Julie Battilana and Tiziana Casciaro

You Need Alone Time

It's all too easy for your days and weeks to fill up with endless meetings. But even when finding time alone to think and reflect feels impossible, you still need to do it. You're a better, more thoughtful leader when you set aside mental space to consider and prepare for tasks—whether it's a new project or yet another meeting.

How can you block out regular chunks of time for reflection?

Adapted from "How CEOs Manage Time,"
by Michael E. Porter and Nitin Nohria

Communicate the Why

When you're sharing plans, strategic goals, or changes with employees, communicating *what* needs to happen and *how* may seem more urgent than explaining the *why*. Maybe the why seems obvious, or the what and how seem sufficient. But the why is what really motivates people—the reason they should support and carry out your plans. Identify the why by answering a few questions: "What's at stake if we do (or don't do) this?" "What will our future look like if we get this done?" Or just ask "So what?" about the initiative you're proposing and keep asking it until you get to the root of the reason you're advocating for a change.

How can you get better at sharing the *why*, rather than just the what and how?

Adapted from "Good Leadership Is About Communicating 'Why,'"
by Nancy Duarte

Maintaining Psychological Safety

Model Healthy Conflict

When we perceive others to be a threat, we're less likely to listen effectively, ask questions, or share our ideas. That's one reason why maintaining psychological safety on your team is so important. One way to build (or rebuild) it is to model healthy conflict. When you and a team member have a disagreement, approach it respectfully by giving the person space to voice their point of view. It's important to welcome and acknowledge opinions that are different from your own, even if it means engaging in civil debate. Doing so shows the rest of your team that it's possible to share opposing perspectives constructively.

Adapted from "Do You Really Trust Your Team?
(And Do They Trust You?)," by Amy Jen Su

Help Your Employees Learn from Each Other

Peer-to-peer learning can be a powerful (and free) development tool. Encourage this kind of learning by setting up a formal program. Start by asking someone on your team (ideally someone with facilitation experience) to oversee the program. Their job is to organize sessions, keep everyone on topic, and maintain a positive atmosphere. Also, set ground rules around honoring confidentiality and accepting feedback graciously, so people feel comfortable sharing. During sessions, tie learning to real-world situations and problems, which will help your employees apply new skills quickly. And encourage people to spread the word so that anyone in the company can get involved.

Adapted from "How to Help Your Employees Learn from Each Other," by Kelly Palmer and David Blake

Don't Be Derailed by Small Stressors

Every day you deal with *microstress*, the result of small setbacks that feel minor and fleeting, but whose effects ripple outward. While microstressors can be hard to spot individually, cumulatively they pack an enormous punch. Think of having to work late because colleagues fell short on a project; it's only another 30 minutes, but the extra effort disrupts your mood and your evening plans and may leave you feeling annoyed tomorrow too. And just like plain old stress, these kinds of stressors can increase your blood pressure and your heart rate, or trigger hormonal or metabolic changes.

What are your small but significant stressors?

Adapted from "The Hidden Toll of Microstress,"
by Rob Cross and Karen Dillon

Learn How Employees Want to Show Commitment

It's easy to assume you know what it looks like when someone cares about their work. But extroverts and introverts demonstrate passion differently, and valuing some displays over others means you aren't treating and rewarding people equally. Talk to employees about how they show enthusiasm, so you'll know what to expect. Maybe some people use energetic body language and speech, while others would rather write about their excitement in a report or share it in one-on-one updates. Aligning your expectations with employees' preferences will help you spot their signs of commitment, especially when their styles don't match yours.

Adapted from "Stop Assuming Introverts Aren't Passionate About Work," by Kai Krautter, Anabel Büchner, and Jon M. Jachimowicz

The Persuasive Power of Scarcity

People value what's scarce. That's why, when you need to be persuasive, an effective approach is to highlight unique benefits and exclusive information. Look for the corporate equivalents of limited-time, limited-supply, or one-of-a-kind offers. If you need a colleague to talk to the boss so a project can move forward, for example, you might point out that the boss is leaving for vacation soon, so the time to act is now. You might also ensure your colleague knows that no one else can give the approval or feedback they need. Emphasizing that a window of opportunity is closing like this can be a good motivator.

———————

Adapted from "Harnessing the Science of Persuasion,"
by Robert B. Cialdini

Managing Employees Who Are More Creative Than You

If some of your employees are creative, overseeing them doesn't require an entirely new approach to management. Start by making sure their creative tendencies fit their role, so you can tap into their full talents. Surround them with detail-oriented project managers who will handle the implementation of their ideas. Reward people for the innovations they come up with. Apply the right amount of pressure to projects—too little will decrease motivation, too much will increase stress. And finally, don't worry if their approach to work is nothing like yours—as long as they're meeting deadlines and accomplishing what they need to.

Adapted from "Motivating Your Most Creative Employees,"
by Tomas Chamorro-Premuzic and Reece Akhtar

Great Mentors Prepare Others to Join Them

Your primary job as a mentor is to pass on your wisdom and expertise. Your secondary job is to identify mentees who have the potential to become mentors and prepare them for that role. To be considered, someone needs true expertise in their area, as well as a generous personality. Talk to candidates about the challenges and satisfactions of the role, including how you analyze problems, consider solutions, and decide how best to help someone. When a person seems ready to make the jump, help them identify their own mentee; you might offer to co-mentor until they feel comfortable. And enjoy their success—it's the ultimate sign that you performed your role well.

Adapted from "6 Things Every Mentor Should Do,"
by Vineet Chopra and Sanjay Saint

Stop Overthinking Tough Problems

Raw intelligence isn't the answer to every problem. When focused thinking isn't getting you anywhere, notice where you're getting stuck; perhaps you've started obsessing over the same answers or approaches. Consider whether experimenting with a new approach, taking a break, or talking through ideas with others might help. And when you do find yourself ruminating, disrupt your thinking with a few minutes of an absorbing activity, such as a puzzle. This can be a surprisingly effective way to break your brain out of a rut.

Adapted from "5 Ways Smart People Sabotage
Their Success," by Alice Boyes

Cross-Train at Work

"Doing more of what you already do well yields only incremental improvement. To get appreciably better at it...work on complementary skills.... You need to engage in the business equivalent of cross-training. If you're technically adept, for instance, delving even more deeply into technical manuals won't get you nearly as far as honing a complementary skill such as communication, which will make your expertise more apparent and accessible to your coworkers.... Developing competency companions works precisely because, rather than simply doing more of the same, you are enhancing how you already behave with new ways of working and interacting that will make that behavior more effective."

Adapted from "Making Yourself Indispensable,"
by John H. Zenger, Joseph Folkman, and Scott Edinger

Questions to Ask Often

I Wonder Why...?

When you ask great questions, you inspire curiosity, creativity, and deeper thinking in yourself and in your employees. One useful question is "I wonder why . . . ?" You have to remain curious about your organization in order to bring new ideas to life. Wondering why something is the way it is may lead to an unsatisfactory answer ("Because we've always done it that way"). But asking "I wonder why . . . ?" is the first step in overcoming the inertia that can stifle growth—because it inevitably leads to the perfect follow-up question: "I wonder if things could be done differently?"

Adapted from "5 Questions Leaders Should Be Asking All the Time,"
by James E. Ryan

During Change, Give People Choices

Organizational change can make employees feel they're at the mercy of forces they have no control over. To reduce their fear and increase their buy-in, give them as many choices about the change as possible. For example, you might work with managers to create a communication plan for what's happening, come up with a timeline for initiating new processes, and highlight team- or unit-specific processes that should stay the same. It's natural for people to view change with skepticism and worry about how their jobs and influence may be negatively affected. Allowing them to make some choices about next steps can build buy-in and increase engagement.

Adapted from "Change Is Hard. Here's How to Make It Less Painful,"
by Erika Andersen

Reward Employees with Time, Not Just Money

People tend to prefer monetary rewards, but helping your employees be savvier about time can increase their job satisfaction. For example, offer incentives that save people time, such as a program where employees can earn points toward services like housecleaning—rather than material items or cash. Put a dollar value on noncash rewards, such as more vacation time. Since we're used to thinking in financial terms (higher versus lower salaries, say), seeing what time-based benefits are "worth" helps us appreciate them more. Marketing time as money in these ways helps people feel that you care about their well-being and their work-life balance, finds research from Harvard Business School.

Adapted from "Time for Happiness,"
by Ashley Whillans

Strong Leaders Don't Hide Their Weaknesses

The best managers have the humility to acknowledge their weaknesses and vulnerabilities. It's tempting to want colleagues to see you only at your best, but that's unrealistic. Why? For one thing, it's unsustainable. We all make mistakes; sooner or later, you will too. For another, leading is about connecting. People will work hard for you if they feel connected to you. And they won't feel that way if you only let them see what you think will impress them. So don't be afraid to own up to your imperfections. Think of it this way: You aren't weak; you have weaknesses. There is a difference.

Adapted from "The Best Leaders Aren't Afraid to
Ask for Help," by Peter Bregman

Don't Be a Victim of Your Success

Look Beyond Titles

To keep performing at your best, you must overcome the barriers that accompany your success. One barrier is being too attached to your job title. Tackling big, complicated problems requires collaboration, cross-disciplinary work, and gathering ideas from across the organization. But if you start thinking that your ideas should take precedence because you're the most senior person in the room, you may alienate the people whose help you need. Solving complex issues requires you to look beyond the title in your email signature and embrace an identity as a change leader.

How might your professional identity be narrowing your view—or hampering your contributions?

Adapted from "Want to Change the World? Don't Let Your Own Success Get in the Way," by Rosabeth Moss Kanter

Your Influence Depends on Your Relationships

"Management begins with you, because who you are as a person, what you think and feel, the beliefs and values that drive your actions, and especially how you connect with others all matter to the people you must influence. Every day those people examine every interaction with you, your every word and deed, to uncover your intentions. They ask themselves, 'Can I trust this person?' How hard they work, their level of personal commitment, their willingness to accept your influence, will depend in large part on the qualities they see in you. . . . It's easy to get those crucial relationships wrong. Effective managers possess the self-awareness and self-management required to get them right."

Adapted from "Are You a Good Boss—or a Great One?"
by Linda A. Hill and Kent Lineback

How to Make Your Employees Quit

Lead with Bias

Losing an employee hurts morale and productivity, and replacing people who leave is expensive. One mistake that can lead your people to quit is leading in unfair, biased ways. If employees see you as biased, it will lower trust, which in turn lowers morale. To avoid this situation, step back to reflect before you make decisions. Consider what's driving you, and whether certain factors (about someone else or you) are influencing you in an unfair way. Are you basing choices on evidence or preference? Are there gaps in your knowledge you need to fill before making the call? Asking for regular feedback from your team—and acting on it—can also help.

Adapted from "8 Things Leaders Do That Make
Employees Quit," by Jon Christiansen

Questions to Ask Yourself

How Do I Lead Under Pressure?

Through the ups and downs of your career, regularly asking yourself a few questions can help you stay on track with your goals and priorities. One of those questions is: How do I behave under pressure? During a crisis, people watch you closely, so be careful about the signals you send. Are you calm or harried? Do you accept responsibility or assign blame? Do you support employees or point fingers? Be thoughtful about when and how pressure affects you.

How do you make sure your behaviors stay consistent with your core values?

Adapted from "What to Ask the Person in the Mirror,"
by Robert Steven Kaplan

Stop Avoiding Hard Decisions

Part of your job is making difficult choices. But leaders often put off making a tough call. Why?

- **You're afraid of disappointing people.** Whether it's delivering bad financial news or announcing a necessary but unpopular change initiative, sometimes you don't want to hurt morale.

- **You're afraid of being wrong.** Many situations you face are complex and ambiguous. It's tempting to gather just a little more data, so you don't look bad if you choose wrong.

- **You're afraid of being seen as unfair.** This is especially an issue if you don't want to be perceived as playing favorites, such as when assigning coveted projects.

Have you let these dynamics prevent timely decision-making?

Adapted from "Leaders, Stop Avoiding Hard Decisions,"
by Ron Carucci

Don't Let Distance Lead to Bad Behavior

Leaders can't know everything that happens in their companies. But sometimes the distance between you and your employees can allow bad behavior to fester, especially if a team's good results seem to signal that everything is fine. That's why you should encourage employees to speak up when they see toxic behavior and create ways for them to easily do it. Clearly demonstrate (and consider documenting) what kind of conduct is acceptable as well as what won't be tolerated. Then, when an employee raises concerns, act on what you've heard. By showing that you'll enforce norms of good conduct, you can build trust and close the distance between you and your employees.

Adapted from "Are You Enabling a Toxic Culture Without Realizing It?," by Celia Swanson

Help Employees Make Better Decisions by Explaining Yours

Requiring your approval over everything isn't healthy for you or your team. To empower employees to make good choices, help them build strong judgment. One approach is to explain your own decisions after you make them. Discuss how you thought about the subjective and objective criteria, the risks and trade-offs, and the key stakeholder considerations. Your transparency will help people better understand the company's priorities and demonstrate what they should consider in their own judgment calls. And when you see someone make a less-than-optimal decision, ask about their thought process to get their perspective, then share what you would have done differently and why.

Adapted from "Do You Really Trust Your Team?
(And Do They Trust You?)," by Amy Jen Su

To Move On from Change

Focus on Your Many Facets

Sometimes a big change—personal or professional—upends your identity. Focusing on the nonwork aspects of yourself can help you move forward. If you were passed over for a long-sought promotion, for example, you may feel angry and disappointed. But your identity is made up of many elements, so throw yourself into the ones you feel good about, such as family and friends, community commitments, or volunteer work. Doing so won't magically take away the hurt, but it can remind you that you care about and enjoy many things beyond your job. Reflecting on your identity's full range will help you center on the positive as you figure out what's next.

Adapted from "When a Major Life Change Upends Your Sense of Self," by Madeline Toubiana, Trish Ruebottom, and Luciana Turchick Hakak

Taking a Stand Doesn't Mean You Have to Pay a Price

"In many stories we hear about workplace courage, the people who fight for positive change end up being ostracized—and sometimes even lose their jobs. . . . My research, though, tells a more nuanced story. Most acts of courage don't come from whistleblowers or organizational martyrs. Instead, they come from respected insiders at all levels who take action—be it campaigning for a risky strategic move, pushing to change an unfair policy, or speaking out against unethical behavior—because they believe it's the right thing to do. Their reputations and track records enable them to make more headway than those on the margins or outside the organization could. And when they manage the process well, they don't necessarily pay a high price for their actions; indeed, they may see their status rise as they create positive change."

Adapted from "Cultivating Everyday Courage,"
by James R. Detert

The Power of Solving Problems

Being a people-focused leader is a worthy approach. But there's much to be said for being a problem-focused one too. Rather than attracting followers through charisma or status, this approach centers on getting others excited to solve key business challenges. You'll need to know how to frame problems so they align with what top talent cares about, which includes identifying areas that are truly important to the company or the world. And while you can still pursue deep expertise, you should gain familiarity with multiple areas to help you make connections. The payoff is leadership that inspires people to do big, hard, bold things.

How can you make problem-focused leadership a part of your style?

Adapted from "The Power of Leaders Who Focus on Solving Problems," by Deborah Ancona and Hal Gregersen

Take Stock of Your Soft Skills

In the age of AI, your soft skills—not digital ones—are what will best support your career growth. To figure out what you need to develop, audit yourself. You're used to highlighting technical abilities on your résumé; which people skills would you do the same for? Think about areas such as communication, adaptability, and conflict resolution, considering which you could cultivate more. Ask colleagues and mentors about your strengths and weaknesses. Then make a plan to nurture specific skills. To enhance your creativity, for instance, you might do anything from taking an improv class to enrolling in a drawing seminar. Whatever your approach, challenge yourself to push beyond your comfort zone.

Adapted from "How to Improve Your Soft Skills as a Remote Worker," by Rebecca Knight

Persuasive Leaders Know How to Compromise

"Persuasion . . . often involves—indeed, demands—compromise. Perhaps that is why the most effective persuaders seem to share a common trait: they are open-minded, never dogmatic. They enter the persuasion process prepared to adjust their viewpoints and incorporate others' ideas. . . . When colleagues see that a persuader is eager to hear their views and willing to make changes in response to their needs and concerns, they respond very positively. They trust the persuader more and listen more attentively. They don't fear being bowled over or manipulated. They see the persuader as flexible and are thus more willing to make sacrifices themselves. [That's why] good persuaders often enter the persuasion process with judicious compromises already prepared."

Adapted from "The Necessary Art of Persuasion,"
by Jay A. Conger

Learning to Learn

Be Vulnerable

Acquiring new knowledge quickly and continually is a skill that will never be obsolete. One way to do it is to be vulnerable enough to learn. If you're an expert in one area, not being good at others may seem unappealing or intimidating. But great learners are willing to feel like beginners. Rather than a mindset of "I'm so bad at this!" take a perspective of "Of course I'm bad—I'm new to it. But I'll get better." The more you allow yourself to make mistakes, ask questions, and seek help from others, the faster you'll build competence in your new skill.

———————————

Adapted from "Learning to Learn,"
by Erika Andersen

Organizational Chaos as a Growth Opportunity

When everything feels in flux due to shifts in leadership or corporate restructurings, your mindset can make all the difference. Rather than giving in to despair or pessimism, find the opportunities in what's happening: How do the changes affect your role? What do they mean for the company's future and your place in it? How could they help you advance in your career or enhance your skills? If the answers aren't clear yet, keep looking for them; choose to see the chaos as a chance to grow, not a barrier to your progress. Staying "heads up" rather than "heads down" will help you navigate the turbulence and emerge from it productively.

Adapted from "How to Stay Grounded Through
Organizational Chaos," by Rebecca Knight

Leading with Integrity Is a Goal That Never Ends

You're a role model when it comes to ethics. If you cut corners, flout the rules, or ignore top performers' bad behavior, you'll give others permission to do the same. But lead with integrity, and you'll inspire employees to follow your example. You'll also show customers (who often care a great deal about how companies do business) what you stand for.

How do you show employees and customers that integrity matters to you?

_____

Adapted from "How to Build a Company That (Actually) Values Integrity," by Robert Chesnut

Get Better at Failure

You have to be able to handle failure well. But around 70% of Americans have a personality type that leads them to react poorly when things go wrong, according to an analysis from Dattner Consulting and Hogan Assessment Systems. For example, some people blame others, others deny there's a problem or that they played a role, and still others place too much blame on themselves.

How do you typically respond to failure? What can you do to respond better?

Adapted from "Managing Yourself: Can You Handle Failure?,"
by Ben Dattner and Robert Hogan

Stay in Learning Mode All the Time

What distinguishes leaders who develop the strongest leadership skills? Staying in learning mode, according to researchers from UNSW Sydney Business School and the University of Michigan. When you're in learning mode, you interpret setbacks to mean you don't yet have all the skills you need, rather than thinking you're unable to overcome a certain challenge. You also avoid constantly comparing yourself to peers, and instead focus on how you've grown and how you can expand your capabilities further. When difficulties come up, simply asking yourself whether you're in learning mode right now can be a powerful cue to consider what the situation can teach you.

Adapted from "Good Leaders Are Good Learners,"
by Lauren A. Keating, Peter A. Heslin,
and Susan (Sue) Ashford

Leading Well Is a Journey of Years

"Too often managers underestimate how much time and effort it takes to keep growing and developing. Becoming a great boss is a lengthy, difficult process of learning and change, driven mostly by personal experience. Indeed, so much time and effort are required that you can think of the process as a journey—a journey of years. What makes the journey especially arduous is that the lessons involved cannot be taught. Leadership is using yourself as an instrument to get things done in the organization, so it is about self-development. There are no secrets and few shortcuts. You and every other manager must learn the lessons yourself, based on your own experience as a boss."

Adapted from "Are You a Good Boss—or a Great One?," by Linda A. Hill and Kent Lineback